Gently God Comforts

MARIE SHROPSHIRE

HARVEST HOUSE PUBLISERS
Eugene, Oregon 97402

Gently God Comforts
Copyright © 1998 by Marie Shropshire
Published by Harvest House Publishers
Eugene, Oregon 97402

Library of Congress Cataloging-in-Publication Data

Shropshire, Marie, 1921–
    Gently God comforts / Marie Shropshire.
        p.   cm.
    ISBN 1-56507-778-4
    1. Devotional calendars.   2. Consolation.   I. Title.
BV4811.S3783   1998
242'.4—dc21.   97-44715
                                                        CIP

Whatever the season,
whatever the month,
whatever the day,
wherever you are,
you can know you are
on a journey with God.

Contents

Words of Peace

I Embrace the New

Lord, You're about to fling open the door to a new era in my life. As I say goodbye to the old, I embrace the new.

As You close the door to the past, please let me glance back long enough to say thank You for Your specific help in the experiences of my past.

You manifested Your presence when I felt lonely and forsaken. You held my hand and assured me that the darkness would pass. Thank You, Lord.

You guided me when I stood at the crossroads wondering which direction to take. Your Spirit pointed out the way.

Lord, before I close my own personal door to the past, I want to be sure I'm leaving the house clean. Forbid that I should drag any garbage into the future or perhaps even worse, bury it behind.

If I bury doubts, fears, resentments, or unforgiveness, they will spring up later to haunt and endanger me. So, as I enter the door to the new year, let me deal with any negatives. Give me the courage to face things I've hidden or ignored. Let me not blame others, but take responsibility for my own reactions.

I invite You into any dark places within me. Point out what I've refused to face. Give me the fearlessness to walk with You into those areas of my hidden self. Then grant me the patience to work out what needs working out. I yield myself to You. Cleanse me. Prepare me for what lies ahead.

Lord, as You swing open the door to the new year, I'm glad You can see ahead, because I can't. It's as if I'm staring into fog. But if I could see ahead, I might be afraid. Or I might be tempted to tell You how to change things.

I thank You, Lord, that You not only *know* the way ahead, but you have also *planned* the way. And I know it is good because You are a God of wisdom and love. When trials and unpleasant experiences unfold, remind me that You're in charge and that You work everything out for my good—and especially for my spiritual growth.

As You open the door to the new year, I open the door to my heart. I want to open the door widely enough that the wind of Your Spirit can blow freely through me. Sweep away any cobwebs of self-doubt. Remind me of who I am in Christ. Refresh my memory. Through Your power, I can do everything You require of me.

I open my personal door, that I may hear You say to me as You said to Joshua, "As I was with Moses, so I will be with you; I will never leave you nor forsake you. Be strong and courageous" (Joshua 1:5,6). I choose to accept Your challenge.

I open my door and hear You say to me as You said to Gideon in his weakness: "The Lord is with you, mighty warrior" (Judges 6:12). I choose to believe You and to undertake whatever you decree.

I open the door more widely and hear You speak through Paul: "Rejoice in the Lord always" (Philippians 4:4). Lord, I choose to rejoice in You more in the year ahead than I did in the past year. Help me not to center my attention on circumstances, but upon You. If I look at circumstances, I may become despondent. If I focus on You, I'll know You are in charge, and I can rejoice regardless of circumstances.

Yes, Lord, You are flinging open the door to the new year. But as I try to see ahead, I see only a little more than a cloud of vapor. However, that is enough. I have goals and dreams. As I follow Your leading, your light will shine and the vapor will disappear. I will pursue goals which I believe are Your desire for me.

As I step over the threshold, I have one last request. It's for those hurting ones to whom the fog looks ominously dense. Let Your light shine through me to them. Make me a channel of love, light, and warmth. Let me take their hand and lead them into the new year. And maybe at the end of their journey they will pause and say, "Lord, let me glance back long enough to say thank You."

Words
of
Expectancy

1

Finding Our Dreams

Whatever your hand finds to do, do it with all
your might (Ecclesiastes 9:10).

The dream of a certain little boy was to sing in the children's choir. When he was finally selected, he wrote a letter to God: "Dear God, at last I've made the children's choir. Now You can hear me sing every Sunday." The little boy was elated because his dream had been fulfilled.

This is a good time for you and me to uncover our dreams. Let's discover the desires and goals the Lord has placed in our hearts. Our Father has something new for our lives. Paul says we have been redeemed so that we might habitually "live and behave in newness of life" (Romans 6:4 AMP). To live habitually in newness of life is to experience the unfolding of new dreams.

Oswald Chambers advises, "Continually restate to yourself what the purpose of your life is." The purpose of our lives will influence the goals we set for ourselves this year. But we need to "continually restate" to ourselves our dreams and purposes. Unless we keep our dreams before us, reviewing them regularly, we may be apt to veer offtrack and allow other interests to keep us from reaching our highest goals.

Keeping our God-given goals before us will fortify us in times of discouragement. Future success requires that we keep our eyes on our goal, giving no heed to delays and setbacks. The little boy who finally made it into the children's choir had to endure a period of waiting. Meanwhile, he grew and practiced.

"He who observes the wind [and waits for all conditions to be favorable] will not sow," says Solomon, "and he who regards the clouds will not reap" (Ecclesiastes 11:4 AMP). If we wait for everything to be in our favor before setting out on the road to achievement, we'll probably never reap a harvest.

While sowing, however, we must remember that God not only planted the dreams in our hearts, but it is He who is working through us. Norman Grubb reminds us in his book *The Spontaneous You* that we are the "human means by which God is doing His own work—and that's all." Without this understanding, we are subject to being caught up "in that frustrating, ulcer-causing, nervous-breakdown-producing rat race of 'doing our best for Him.'" The God who speaks gently would have us avoid that.

When we give ourselves to a project, we're to recognize that it is God at work within us, not we ourselves apart from Him. Even while pursuing big dreams and moving toward our goals, we can rest in God.

Some of us have difficulty achieving balance in our work. We may recall Horace Mann's gem: "Lost, somewhere between sunrise and sunset, two golden hours, each set with sixty diamond minutes. No reward is offered, for they are gone forever."

Paul set an example for us when he said, "I keep going on, grasping ever more firmly that purpose for which Christ Jesus grasped me. . . . I leave the past behind and with hands outstretched to whatever lies ahead, I go straight for the goal" (Philippians 3:12-14 PHILLIPS).

Without doubt, Paul accomplished more than any other man of his day. But he did it by knowing that it was not he but Christ in him. As long as we're guided by the Holy Spirit, we can safely regard our dreams as from God.

The Lord wants to put dreams in our hearts. Daring to dream big dreams will keep us from becoming hopeless victims of spiritual paralysis. And it will keep us from slipping into joyless living.

However dismal our prospects may be, let's remember Paul's words: "Don't worry over anything whatever; tell God every detail of your needs in earnest and thankful prayer" (Philippians 4:6 PHILLIPS).

2

No Excess Baggage

*This is the day the LORD has made; let us rejoice
and be glad in it (Psalm 118:24).*

We have embarked on an extended journey.
This is a gift from God—a journey into
the next year of our lives. This year holds
365 days, crediting us with more than a thousand minutes per day.

Before we journey far into this year, we want to be
sure we're not bringing any excess baggage, such as negative attitudes, hurts, or resentments. We want to hand
those over to God. Of course, problems and difficulties
have to be worked out and walked through. We cannot
change what happened to us last year. But we can
change our response to those happenings.

Several years ago when an American couple was
visiting Rome on New Year's Eve, they discovered a
strange tradition—to throw something out the window at midnight. Worn-out clothing and broken furniture came crashing from windows all over the city at
the stroke of midnight.

Maybe that tradition is not so strange. You and I may own some useless clutter in the form of unpleasant memories which we have a habit of dwelling on. Any unhealthy mental or emotional baggage can take up valuable space needed for spiritual treasures.

"Our greatest treasures are wrapped up in the things that can't be kept in a safety deposit box," says Tim Kimmel in his book *Little House on the Freeway*. When I don't take enough time for God or myself, I deprive myself of valuable treasures. I may be placing a greater price tag on material things than God does. I want to pay attention when God says, "Slow down—you're about to miss some of the beauty I've planned for you."

Little children have much to teach us in this area. When my oldest granddaughter was a toddler, she and her parents lived in Denver, Colorado. One winter day when my son and I were talking on the telephone, he asked, "Susan, do you want to talk to Grandmommy?"

Captivated by the beauty of the season's first snowfall, Susan came to the phone only long enough to wisely say, "I don't have time to talk. I have to watch it snow."

How much more tranquil would be our life's journey if we, like little children, would dare to say *no* to the less important matters and take time to revel in God's handiwork.

When I stand and gaze at the early-morning pink-and-silver clouds in the east, or the crimson-and-gold sky in the west at sunset, I am awed by the beauty of God's creation. Elizabeth Barrett Browning must have known how to journey through life at God's pace, enjoying His creation, for she wrote these immortal lines:

> *Earth's crammed with heaven,*
> *And every common bush afire with God;*
> *But only he who sees takes off his shoes;*
> *The rest sit round and pluck blackberries.*

Dare we believe that every common bush is afire with God? As we journey through this year, will we see His beauty, reverence Him, and hear His voice in the common and ordinary?

Taking time for God ensures a safe journey. We'll travel over some rough places, but the Lord has traveled every mile before us. He knows the way we should take, and He will be with us.

3

Joyous Expectancy

*All these blessings will come upon you and
accompany you if you obey the LORD your God
(Deuteronomy 28:2).*

It's one thing for us to realize that another
year lies before us. It's quite another to
enter this year with joyous expectancy.
The Lord wants to favor us with blessings this year. We
are His beloved children, and His desire is to set us free
from every bondage and pour out His love upon us in
tangible ways.

This morning I picked up a new book and read the
flyleaf. Two sentences struck me as counsel that could
help me live more expectantly this year: "Embrace each
day as a gift to be treasured. Discover anew that God is
at work not only in the momentous events of life but
also in the quiet times, pouring out His tender mercies
in unending streams of love."

How often I overlook the little everyday things that
God means for blessing. How often I fail to see His

21

hand at work in everything that concerns me. How prone I am to forget that the blessings God promised in His Word are for me today.

To be blessed does not mean we escape life's trials. But we learn how to live through them triumphantly, expecting God to be with us. The psalmist asked, "Why should I fear when evil days come?" (Psalm 49:5). When we read the books of Samuel, Kings, and Chronicles, we see that David experienced all kinds of trials. But he faced them fearlessly, knowing that God would see him safely through.

The Lord promises, "Call upon me in the day of trouble; I will deliver you" (Psalm 50:15). Having that assurance, we can live expectantly, regardless of what comes. We can rest in the truth of the words of Annie Johnson Flint:

> *God has not promised skies always blue,*
> *Flower-strewn pathways all our lives through;*
> *God has not promised sun without rain,*
> *Joy without sorrow, peace without pain.*
>
> *But God has promised strength for the day,*
> *Rest for the labor, light for the way,*
> *Grace for the trials, help from above,*
> *Unfailing sympathy, undying love.*

Lloyd Ogilvie introduces his book *Turn Your Struggles into Stepping Stones* with this illustration: One night he had to wade across a raging river by carefully stepping from stone to stone. At last safely across, he realized that life is like that. "In the raging river of life's struggles, the Lord provides us with stepping stones."

With that same assurance, you and I can live expectantly, trusting the Lord to guide us safely through anything the future holds.

As we think of living expectantly, our expectations are to be in God alone. Most of us have discovered that putting our expectations in others often leads to disappointment. One man went so far as to say that his unhappiness is in direct proportion to what he expects of others.

Many of us expect too much not only of others but of ourselves as well. Making impossible demands on ourselves leads to unhappiness and frustration. Pastor/author Judson Edwards says that while we are praying for inner peace and joy, and buying books on happiness, we are living in destructive, stress-producing ways. He says the truest test of our faith is in "our capacity to laugh, to treasure life, and to celebrate God's goodness."

Treasuring life and celebrating God's goodness enables us to live expectantly. Basking in God's goodness, we can accept ourselves as God accepts us in Christ, knowing that we will make mistakes, but knowing also that God is bigger than any mistake we can make. We may become disillusioned with ourselves, but God never does.

Putting our expectations in ourselves instead of in God causes us to live in what has been described as the *bumblebee syndrome*. When I flit from one task to another like a bumblebee, I can be sure I'm putting my expectations in myself instead of trusting God to direct me. Judson Edwards says, "The bumblebee approach to life has been tried by millions of good Christians and found to be a sure way to ungodly exhaustion."

Our culture seems to expect everyone to win all the time. But failure is a part of life. Life has setbacks and losses. God does not expect us to be perfect but faithful. We live with joyous expectancy when we recognize that all of us are human, and that we can accept ourselves and each other as we are. God has chosen to bless us simply because we are His.

People of Bible times had the same challenges as you and I do. Once when Moses was leading the Israelites through their wilderness wanderings he was talking to God, and God answered, "I will do the very thing you have asked, because I am pleased with you and I know you by name" (Exodus 33:17).

You and I are as much the children of God as Moses was, and we are no less loved. Sometimes we wonder how the Lord can be pleased with us, because we focus on our faults and presume that God does too. But if we have accepted His gift of salvation, He looks at us through the shed blood of Jesus and loves us unconditionally. When we remember that, how can we do other than live expectantly?

God's desire for us is that we live in the confident assurance that He is in control. As we dream and set goals, asking the Lord's guidance, we can expect Him to be with us. Let's begin this next year of our lives expecting the Lord's richest blessings!

Words
of
Love

4

The Language of Love

*By this all men will know that you are my
disciples, if you love one another
(John 13:35).*

"The language that God hears best is the silent language of love," said a saint of another century. Meditating recently on that thought, I was impressed with the idea that the language all of us need most to hear and feel is the language of love.

The language of love is not necessarily words spoken, but love *demonstrated*, proved by our actions. This kind of love is deeper than words. Words can be empty and artificial. The silent language of love comes from the depths of one's being. It travels on thought waves. It is prompted by what we feel at the core of our being. The quality of love is determined, of course, by the character of the one who loves.

God, whose character is perfect, demonstrated His own perfect love for us by sending His Son to be perfect love on earth. By Jesus' life, He showed us how to love one another. John declared:

Whoever does not love does not know God, because God is love. This is how God showed his love among us: He sent his one and only Son into the world that we might live through him. . . . God lives in us and his love is made complete in us. . . . We love because he first loved us (1 John 4:8,9,12,19).

Jesus' entire life was spent in self-giving love. He manifested love in everything He said and did. He longed for His followers to live in love. Paul indicated his grasp of the value of love when he wrote, "The object and purpose of our instruction and charge is love, which springs from a pure heart" (1 Timothy 1:5 AMP).

The word *love* appears almost 600 times in the Bible. You and I may use the word several times a day, but more important than *speaking* the word "love" is *living* love. Nothing can compare with giving and receiving genuine love.

In his book *Love and Living*, Thomas Merton defines love as "an intensification of life, a completeness, a fullness, a wholeness of life." He said, "Love is not just something that happens to you: It is a certain way of being alive." We can understand this truth better when we remember that God Himself is love and life.

We become more fully alive and more self-giving when we more completely accept God's love for us. Being fully aware of God's love makes us not only more loving but more accepting—of others, of ourselves, and of all God's creation.

In today's world where outside influences threaten our security, many of us yearn for an extra measure of affirmation. We need the assurance that we are unconditionally loved and accepted. We long to be reminded that we are loved just as we are, with all our shortcomings and limitations—that we are valuable in God's sight. And He does this perfectly. All He asks is that we spend time with Him and receive His unconditional love.

5

The Practice of Love

Greet one another with a kiss of love
(1 Peter 5:14).

Throughout the Old and New Testaments we read of people showing affection for one another. "Laban kissed his grandchildren and his daughters" as he told them goodbye (Genesis 31:55). "Orpah kissed her mother-in-law goodbye" as Naomi left for Bethlehem (Ruth 1:14). "The king [David] kissed Absalom," his son (2 Samuel 14:33).

The writers of the New Testament did not hesitate to express the importance of expressing physical affection. They understood the need for touch. Paul closed four of his letters with the instruction to "greet one another with a holy kiss."

The father of the prodigal "ran to his son, threw his arms around him and kissed him" (Luke 15:20). Jesus praised the penitent woman for caressing His feet (Luke 7:44-50). One present-day advocate of touching goes so far as to say, "A simple caress has the potential of changing a whole life."

Few of us doubt the importance of caressing small children. But many of us are not aware of the continuing need for frequent loving touches throughout life. Some medical doctors have discovered that demonstrated affection is essential at every stage of life.

Dr. David Bressler of UCLA is one such doctor. He gives many of his patients a homework assignment: "I write out a formal prescription that says simply, 'Four hugs a day—without fail.'" Dr. Bressler says we should never underestimate "how powerful this therapy can be."

Dr. Harold Voth agrees. "Hugging can lift depression—enabling the body's immune system to become tuned up," says Dr. Voth. "Hugging breathes fresh life into a tired body. . . . In the home, daily hugging will strengthen relationships and significantly reduce friction."

Little children were brought to Jesus for Him to place His hands on them and bless them. Many times His hands touched the suffering and they were healed. The hands of Jesus always communicated love.

Jesus has bestowed His love upon us. His is a special kind of love that can flow through our hands to bring comfort to the lonely, healing to the hurting, or encouragement to the downcast, or can simply convey love and acceptance. The more we practice pure love, the more the love of God is perfected in us.

6

The Springs of Love

Love is patient, love is kind. . . . Love never fails. . . . And now these three remain: faith, hope and love. But the greatest of these is love (1 Corinthians 13:4,8,13).

Many sailors have been encouraged by the flashing signal from Minot's light off Scituate, Massachusetts. The signal spells "I love you" in nautical code. Several years ago the Coast Guard decided to replace the old equipment. The officials announced that for technical reasons the new machines would be unable to flash the "I love you" message. When the public protested, the Coast Guard found a way to continue sending the message to cheer lonely sailors.

Both young and old need to receive the continual message that we're loved. A little girl went to church with her dad, leaving her mother and newborn baby brother at home. Back at home, her mother asked her, "How was church?"

Her prompt disappointed reply came: "Nobody hugged me."

As God's children, we want to grow continually in our ability to express love to others in every possible way. Many people in today's world are starving for love. Only God's love expressed through you and me can satisfy that hunger.

Oswald Chambers reminds us, "The springs of love are in God, not in us. It is absurd to look for the love of God in our hearts naturally; it is only there when it has been shed abroad in our hearts by the Holy Spirit."

We can show genuine love to others only when we are certain that God loves us. God has no measuring stick by which He determines whether we are lovable. He loves us simply because He is love and because we belong to Him. He delights in our coming to Him to receive a greater and greater awareness of His love. The more we accept His love, the more we are transformed into His likeness.

Minister/author Dr. Charles Stanley writes, "God's sole intent is to reveal His love for you. And while He desires your love in return, He is committed to not pressuring you into a relationship with Himself. . . . Just as God came to earth to seek a personal relationship with us, we too must seek His love above everything else."

Jesus sits at the right hand of the Father, interceding for us, loving us, knowing our every need even before we ask. He takes pleasure in our coming to Him with our needs, our doubts, our fears, and our questions. He never says, "You're not worthy to come to the Father." If we have accepted Jesus as our personal Savior, we have been made worthy through Jesus. He wants us to know He delights in us and in our fellowship.

We are unable, like the first disciples, to walk down literal streets with the physical Jesus as we talk with Him. But we can enjoy intimate fellowship with Him just as His first disciples did. When we contemplate His love and meditate on the Scriptures (not simply read the words of Scripture), we can experience Him in our hearts and know Him more fully.

"When the Holy Spirit has shed abroad the love of God in our hearts, then that love requires cultivation," says Oswald Chambers. "No love on earth will develop without being cultivated. We have to dedicate ourselves to love, which means identifying ourselves with God's interests in other people."

The better we know the Lord, the more we love Him. When we see Him as He really is, we cannot resist His love. And we are eager to share that love.

The well-known preacher Charles Spurgeon wrote, "No joy on earth is equal to the bliss of being all taken up with love to Christ. If I had my choice of all the lives that I could live, I certainly would not choose to be an emperor, nor to be a millionaire, nor to be a philosopher, for power and wealth and knowledge bring with them sorrow. But I would choose to have nothing to do but to love my Lord Jesus—nothing, I mean, but to do all things for His sake, and out of love to him."

Before we can say as Spurgeon did that we desire only to love God and to do His will, we must come to a deep realization that God loves us personally and individually. We know He loves us not only because Jesus said so or because the Bible says so, or because it's our opinion, but because we accept His love by faith and interiorize this truth, making it a part of our very being.

All of us are familiar with the love verses in 1 Corinthians chapter 13, but have you read that passage in *The Message* translation of the New Testament?

Love never gives up.
Love cares more for others than for self.
Love doesn't want what it doesn't have.
Love doesn't strut,
Doesn't have a swelled head,
Doesn't force itself on others,
Doesn't revel when others grovel,
Takes pleasure in the flowering of truth,
Puts up with anything,
Trusts God always,
Always looks for the best,
Never looks back,
But keeps going to the end.

When my aunt was serving as a missionary in China, she read the above passage, then asked her listeners to read it for themselves and to try substituting their names in place of the word *love*. After a short time they answered, "It doesn't work."

How right they were! Only God Himself has (and is) such perfect love. But the closer we walk with God, the more of His love we are able to reflect.

Emmett Fox wrote: "There is no difficulty that enough love will not conquer; no disease that enough love will not heal; no door that enough love will not open; no gulf that enough love will not bridge; no wall that enough love will not throw down; no sin that enough love will not redeem."

Of course, only God's love can do all that. May we never limit His love. May we accept it as He gives it and pass it on to others.

7

God's Love for Us

*Who shall separate us from the love of Christ?.... I am
convinced that neither death nor life ... nor anything
else in all creation will be able to separate us from
the love of God that is in Christ Jesus our Lord
(Romans 8:35,38,39).*

All the way my Savior leads me;
What have I to ask beside?
Can I doubt His tender mercy,
Who thro' life has been my guide?

How easy to sing those words and mean them
when all is going well! But when we're faced with trials, such words may sound meaningless. The blind
Fanny J. Crosby penned those lines. She was blind from
the time she was six weeks old. But she composed more
than 6000 hymns, many of which have to do with
God's love and faithfulness.

Every time I read the account of Jesus' crucifixion, I
am struck again by the incredible love that God has for
you and me. To allow His beloved Son to experience

the humiliation and suffering of the cross, our Father certainly has infinite love for us.

In his book *Knowing You Are Loved*, pastor/author John Guest writes, "The Great Lover not only loves you, but he longs for you to know that he loves you. He longs for you to experience his love. . . . He wants to reveal himself to us. He wants to help us to know and abide in a living experience of his love for us."

If we doubt the love and wisdom of God, we may be like the little boy who decided to take matters into his own hands and work out his problems himself. When he discovered that his mother and grandmother had gone for a walk in the woods, leaving him behind, he determined to go and find them.

The child's father didn't try to stop him, but he secretly followed in the distance. After plodding along for about a mile, the little boy turned around, lost and frightened, and began to cry. His father stepped up beside him to comfort him and lead him home.

Our heavenly Father may let us go our own way without restraining us. When we give up and realize we can't find our way alone, the Father makes His presence known. He doesn't scold us but takes our hand and shows us the way to go. God in His gentle love never forces Himself upon us, but He is always faithful.

Lack of trust in God originated in the Garden of Eden. Satan appeared and intimated to Eve that God did not love her—that He was withholding something good from her. Eve listened and partook of the fruit which God had forbidden her and Adam to eat.

The tempter still makes suggestions that God's decisions are unfair or that God doesn't really love us. So subtle are the enemy's tactics that we're often unaware that it's *his* voice causing us to doubt God's love.

Dr. Guest says, "God shows his love for us in creating us. He shows his love for us in redeeming us. He shows his love for us in sanctifying us. Do you see that everything, from start to finish in our lives, is wrapped up in God's love?"

The steadfast love of God endures forever. Absolutely nothing can separate us from His love.

Words
of
Hope

8

The Strength of Hope

*Against all hope, Abraham in hope believed
and so became the father of many nations*
(Romans 4:18).

Without hope, we would have difficulty responding positively to a lot of things that come our way. But with the psalmist we can affirm to the Lord, "My hope is in you" (Psalm 39:7). Because He lives in us, we dare to have confidence in our lives. Without Him we can do nothing, but with Him all things are possible.

Hope energizes us so that we can keep moving in spite of setbacks and disappointments. We can hardly read the Bible without recognizing that the men who succeeded were those who continually hoped in spite of delays and disappointments.

"If your hopes are being disappointed just now it means that they are being purified," says Oswald Chambers. "There is nothing noble the human mind has ever hoped for or dreamed of that will not be fulfilled."

When Nehemiah and his men rebuilt the walls around Jerusalem, they repeatedly met with enemy opposition which would have stopped the fainthearted. But their hope in God spurred them on until their task was completed. (See Nehemiah chapters 2 through 6.)

You and I probably have some walls we would like to rebuild. With our hope in God, we can accomplish our goals. When we feel doubtful about our ability to do what needs to be done, let's declare with the psalmist:

> The LORD is my light and my salvation—whom shall I fear? The LORD is the stronghold of my life—of whom shall I be afraid?... The LORD is my strength and my shield; my heart trusts in him, and I am helped (Psalm 27:1; 28:7).

Quoting Oswald Chambers again; "Some people believe in an omnipotence with no character; they are shut up in a destiny of hopelessness; Jesus can open the door of release and let them right out."

When the staff members of the famous Menninger Foundation were asked to identify the most important ingredient needed by the emotionally disturbed, they unanimously replied, "Hope." Regardless of the smallness or greatness of our problems, hope may be the most important ingredient in our lives. Whatever this year may bring to us, let's hold onto hope—hope in the God who is *for* us.

If our hope seems small, we might do well to reflect on the poem someone found in a cellar on a wall in Cologne, Germany, after World War II:

I BELIEVE

I believe in the sun,
even when it is not shining;
I believe in love,
even when I feel it not;
I believe in God,
even when He is silent.

9

Our Source of Hope

Why are you downcast, O my soul? Why so disturbed
within me? Put your hope in God, for I will yet praise
him, my Savior and my God (Psalm 42:11).

"Home! Home!" chirped my toddler as she
darted from room to room. We had
been away for several days, and her joy
in being back home was boundless. Many of us often
say when we return home from a vacation, "The best
part was getting back home."

Our homes are meant to offer a sense of comfort,
serenity, hope, and well-being. Homes where God's
love and peace reign are much more than a roof over
our heads.

Regardless of the outer structure of our physical
abode, we can always have God as our source of hope.
The psalmist declared, "Lord, you have been our
dwelling place throughout all generations" (Psalm
90:1). Our loving Father offers hope and tranquillity in
His dwelling place.

When we make the Lord our dwelling place, we are not only promised hope but a place of rest and protection. The psalmist said, "He who dwells in the shelter of the Most High will rest in the shadow of the Almighty" (Psalm 91:1). Most often the Lord is the only place where we can find genuine rest. Circumstances are not of our choosing. We deal with unanswered questions and insurmountable problems.

We cannot escape the fact that we live in a fallen world. And what touches others often touches us. The Lord understands that fact, and throughout His Word He offers words of hope and encouragement. Someone said, "Life in Christ is endless hope; without Him it is a hopeless end."

The writer of the book of Hebrews encourages us with these words: "We have this hope as an anchor for the soul, firm and secure" (Hebrews 6:19).

Knowing his certainty of hope in Christ, hymn-writer R. H. McDaniel wrote:

> I'm possessed of a hope that is steadfast and sure,
> Since Jesus came into my heart!
> And no dark clouds of doubt now my pathway obscure,
> Since Jesus came into my heart!

In these last days before the Lord's return, the enemy of our soul is working overtime, trying to destroy our hope. One of his favorite tactics is to plant seeds of doubt in our minds. But we need not fall for his lies and his attempts of deception.

There is always hope. We can declare to the Lord with the psalmist, "My hope is in you" (Psalm 39:7).

10

The Higher Plane of Hope

I wait for the LORD, my soul waits,
and in his word I put my hope (Psalm 130:5).

The psalmist often declared his hope in the Lord, as in the above verse. You and I are prone to forget that the Lord is present in all things, and that we can therefore hope in Him at all times. Wherever we are and whatever we do, the Lord is with us. His hand is upon us to lead us and direct us, to protect and care for us.

When we accepted the Lord as our personal Savior, He came into our hearts and made us His very own. But we can keep on receiving Him more fully as we continue learning more and more about Him. We receive Him more deeply into every area of life.

My college Bible professor illustrated our salvation experience by making a dot on the chalkboard. He said, "That's instantaneous salvation. You've been born again. You've received Jesus into your heart. You've been saved." Then he drew a line the full length of the chalkboard and said, "But in another sense, you keep on being saved."

We young people thought we clearly understood what our wise old professor was saying. But I'm sure most us of are still growing in our understanding of the meaning of continuous salvation.

Minister/author Jon Eargle explains the new birth as being like a snapshot, and continuous salvation as like an unending motion picture. Christian growth and development is an unending process, a journey of faith.

"Faith is our gaze upon a saving God," wrote A. W. Tozer. "It is not a once-done act, but a continuous gaze of the heart at the triune God. . . . When the habit of inward gazing Godward becomes fixed within us, we shall be ushered into a new level of spiritual life."

When we catch a glimpse of that "new level of spiritual life," the lower planes of living no longer satisfy us. Having experienced a higher plane, we begin to understand why David said, "One thing I ask of the LORD, this is what I seek: that I may dwell in the house of the LORD all the days of my life, to gaze upon the beauty of the LORD and to seek him in his temple" (Psalm 27:4). David didn't mean, of course, that he wanted to move into the physical building and live there, but he wanted to have the Lord as his inner dwelling place.

A. W. Tozer said, "If we cooperate with Him in loving obedience, God will manifest Himself to us, and that manifestation will be the difference between a nominal Christian life and a life radiant with the light of His face."

11

Our Hope in God

Why are you downcast, O my soul? Why so disturbed within me? Put your hope in God, for I will yet praise him . . . (Psalm 42:5).

*D*avid often experienced times of discouragement. Once when everything seemed to be going against him, David deplored, "My tears have been my food day and night, while men say to me all day long, 'Where is your God?'" (Psalm 42:3). But David almost always bounced back by talking to himself, reminding himself to put his hope in God.

Most of us can identify with David's low moods. Maybe we should try David's pattern by talking to ourselves in a biblical way. Whether we realize it or not, we talk to ourselves almost constantly, not necessarily audibly but internally.

We used to make jokes about people who talked to themselves, but now we've learned that the right kind of self-talk can enrich our lives. It can help us rise above our feelings and get to our spiritual center.

When our self-talk is sullen or grumpy, we are cooperating with the lower part of ourselves. We are sometimes our own worst enemy. But we need not give in to doubt or despair. We can put our hope in God, and stop warring against ourselves.

When I allow my feelings to take control of me, I may fall into a trap of negative thinking and talking. I once heard someone begin her day by saying, "This is going to be a horrible day. I can feel it." She was indulging in negative self-talk.

Someone asks, "If it's true, why not express it?" Because negative thoughts and words often become self-fulfilling prophecies. Besides, negative thoughts almost always affect our bodies. They also have the power to depress us.

When we see a challenging day ahead, it helps to begin the day by talking to ourselves encouragingly. I like to remind myself that "I can do everything through him who gives me strength" (Philippians 4:13), and that "if God is for us, who can be against us?" (Romans 8:31). Paul declared these truths. So can you and I.

Solomon said, "An anxious heart weighs a man down" (Proverbs 12:25). How often you and I have felt weighed down by anxious feelings. We can relieve our anxious hearts by talking to ourselves encouragingly. Since our lives belong to God, we need not doubt that He is in charge of every situation that we yield to Him.

12

Hope Renewed

*Lord, what do I look for? My hope is in you. . . .
For you have been my hope, O Sovereign LORD, my
confidence since my youth (Psalm 39:7;71:5).*

A speaker stood before a group and asked
for Scripture quotations on faith, hope,
and love. Several persons quoted verses
on faith and love, but few could think of any Scriptures
related to hope. The speaker said, "It seems we have
plenty of love and faith but very little hope."

That may be true of many people today. We look
about us and observe evil all around. We hear forecasts
of doom, and we wonder if there is any reason for hope.
Outside of Christ there is none, but thankfully, in Him
there is abundant hope. God has not changed since He
gave the promises of hope in the Bible.

The little book of Habakkuk tells about a prophet
who went from doubt to faith and hope. Habakkuk lived
during one of Judah's most critical periods. In the first
few verses of the book, Habakkuk was overwhelmed by

52

circumstances. Evil men, not God, were in control. The land was filled with iniquity and violence.

In despair, Habakkuk cried out to God on behalf of the nation. Disregard for God's laws seemed to continue unchecked in spite of Habakkuk's earnest prayers. But God assured him that he need not wait long for his answer. God reminded him that "the just will live by faith" and that the righteous will be cared for in the day of trouble.

In the end, Habakkuk's faith soared above doubt and fear. He declared, "Though the fig tree does not bud and there are no grapes on the vines, though the olive crop fails and the fields produce no food, though there are no sheep in the pen and no cattle in the stalls, yet I will rejoice in the LORD, I will be joyful in God my Savior" (Habakkuk 3:17,18).

Habakkuk is an example of someone who kept his hope strong by looking beyond circumstances to God. Habakkuk fixed his hope on God and declared, "The Sovereign LORD is my strength; he makes my feet like the feet of a deer, he enables me to go on the heights" (Habbakuk 3:19).

God sees and knows your plight and mine, whatever it may be. He wants to renew our hope. Just as Habakkuk wondered for a while if God heard his prayer, we may wonder why our prayers seem to go unanswered. But we can be assured that God never fails to hear the prayers of His devoted children. When we follow Him, we can wait in hope.

We know that the adversary "prowls around like a roaring lion looking for someone to devour" (1 Peter 5:8). Our spiritual enemy knows how to cause us to doubt and fear. He will do all he can to discourage us and make us want to give up. He knows that if he can make us feel that we're less than we are—beloved children of the heavenly Father—we will be of little service in the Father's kingdom. Besides, he delights in making us miserable simply because we are children of the Most High.

Jesus said, "The thief comes only to steal and kill and destroy; I have come that they may have life, and have it to the full" (John 10:10). The spiritual thief wants to steal our joy, kill our ambitions, and destroy our hope. But John reminds us, "You, dear children, are from God and have overcome them, because the one who is in you is greater than the one who is in the world" (1 John 4:4).

Having abundant life and knowing we are of God doesn't remove us from the world or its trials. But it does make us overcomers, if we hold on to our hope in God. "For he has rescued us from the dominion of darkness and brought us into the kingdom of the Son he loves" (Colossians 1:13).

As God's children we need not begin each day by thinking in despair, "Oh dear, another day to face." We can quickly remind ourselves of (and agree with) the psalmist's words: "This is the day the LORD has made; let us rejoice and be glad in it" (Psalm 118:24). He who makes all our days is our hope for each new day.

Robert Muller must be a man of hope. He says: "Be happy, render others happy, proclaim your joy, love passionately your miraculous life. Do not wait for a better world; be grateful for every moment of life." *

When asked how she dealt with the immense problems of Calcutta, Mother Teresa responded, "I focus on the Lord and not the problems. Then I can deal with the problems, holding the strong hand of Jesus." In the same way, you and I can handle our problems without losing hope. There is always hope in Jesus and His all-powerful name.

---

* Quoted in *The Joyful Noiseletter.*

Words
of
Joy

13

Our Life in Christ

That power is like the working of his mighty strength,
which he exerted in Christ when he raised him from the
dead and seated him at his right hand in the heavenly
realms (Ephesians 1:19,20).

At Easter, we remind ourselves anew of the life that is ours through Christ. When Jesus said, "I am the resurrection and the life," He meant more than we may see at first. He is *our* life, He is *our* resurrection—not only when our bodies are finally resurrected, but here and now. Because He lives, we live. He died that we might live victoriously in this life.

When we accept Christ as Savior, we begin as spiritual infants to understand and rejoice in the significance of the resurrection truth. As we grow in our knowledge of the Lord, we appreciate the resurrection to a greater and greater degree. It becomes more personally ours. And the better we understand the significance of the resurrection, the more exciting it becomes. We need no longer be anxious about either life or death.

Knowing Christ as Savior enables us to join the apostle Paul in saying that he wanted "to know the power outflowing from His resurrection [which it exerts over believers]" (Philippians 3:10 AMP).

I became a Christian when I was 11 years old. From that day on I wanted to live only for the Lord. Alone in my room one Saturday afternoon about a year after receiving Christ, I was reading Scripture in preparation for the Easter Sunday school lesson. I was overcome by a flood of tears as I suddenly realized what it cost Jesus to give me eternal life. That was one more step in my spiritual understanding.

A few decades later, when I returned home from a wonderful five-day retreat, I had an unforgettable experience. For three days I lived in ecstasy, sensing such awareness of my oneness with Jesus that I felt to ask anything of Him would be to separate myself from Him. I savored the truth of the song "He's All I Need." At the end of three days my feet touched earth again and my *feeling* of oneness with resurrection life faded. Yet I *knew* that Jesus was no less real or present with me.

Being human, our feelings fluctuate. Feelings are not to be depended upon in our relationship with Christ. If we pay attention to our feelings instead of to the fact of our union with Christ, we will be tempted to doubt the power of the resurrection in our own personal lives. We never want to stop learning and growing in that understanding, for Jesus always has more to give to us.

With the Lord's resurrection power within us, we can face whatever life offers, and rejoice. We can trust Him with the present and with whatever the future holds. We know that the One who loved us enough to die for us will never fail us in any way.

Oswald Chambers reminds us that "after the moral decision to be identified with Jesus in His death has been made, the resurrection life of Jesus invades every bit of [our] human nature." We need only to be sensitive to His presence and to know that He will empower us for every situation we encounter.

If we are lacking in the joy of the resurrection, it may be that we simply have head knowledge which hasn't moved down deep into our hearts. We receive heart knowledge by being still in the Lord's presence, letting Him speak on a level beyond what we can hear, simply by reading our Bibles or praying. Prayer includes listening.

That Saturday afternoon when I experienced tears as I realized the price Jesus paid for my salvation, I was feeling His sorrow without feeling His joy. I hadn't moved on to the joy of the resurrection. I hadn't seen that it was "for the joy set before him [that he] endured the cross" (Hebrews 12:2). There is a time to know His sorrow, but He would also have us move beyond sorrow to the *joy* of His resurrection.

14

His Life Is Our Life

*As in Adam all die, so in Christ all will be made
alive. . . . Death has been swallowed up in victory
(1 Corinthians 15:22,54).*

A certain minister announced that on the
following Sunday he would preach a sermon on heaven. During the week he
received a letter from an elderly man who was quite ill.
The letter read, "I am very interested in the land you're
going to preach about. I have a clear title to a bit of that
land. The donor purchased it for me at a tremendous
sacrifice."

We need to be reminded of the tremendous sacrifice Jesus paid for our salvation: *He gave His life that we
might live.* Then He arose from the grave and ascended
to the Father. Because of His death and resurrection,
we have eternal life.

Like many of you, I learned early in life that Jesus
loves me. But sometimes when we've known a truth all
our lives, we take it for granted. We fail to appreciate it
as fully as those to whom the message is brand-new.

Easter is a good time for us to reflect on the meaning of the cross and the victory that Jesus won for us there.

Remember the story of the two men on the road to Emmaus after the crucifixion? Their hopes had been dashed when Jesus was crucified. Their ears had been too dull to grasp the message Jesus had been telling them—that He would rise again. When Jesus appeared to them, they were filled with excitement as they realized who He was and that He had risen. You and I need to be filled with a new excitement as we meditate today on the Lord's love and resurrection power.

This resurrection power is the same today as in the days of the disciples. God the Father inhabits our hearts through His indwelling presence. When I am tempted to be discouraged, I need to remind myself that I have been bought with a price, and because of this, I belong to Christ and He is with me, within me, and for me.

Before the disciples knew that Jesus had risen from the grave, they felt so hopeless and discouraged that life seemed useless. You and I know He is risen, but sometimes we allow discouragement to overtake us. Many things happen to cause doubts to rise in our hearts. We find ourselves taking our eyes off Jesus, the only One who can deliver us from our doubts and discouragements.

We will never be able to understand why certain tragedies happen. But we can be assured that God knows and understands our hurts. That's part of the resurrection message.

Sometimes it's in life's ruin and rubble that we see the cross of Christ most clearly. Tradition has it that it was the sight of a huge cross amidst the ruins of a cathedral off the coast of China that inspired seventeenth-century John Bowring to write the hymn "In the Cross of Christ I Glory."

In the cross of Christ I glory,
Towering o'er the wrecks of time;
All the light of sacred story
Gathers 'round its head sublime.

When the woes of life o'ertake me,
Hopes deceive, and fears annoy,
Never shall the cross forsake me:
Lo! It glows with peace and joy.

Apart from Christ we have nothing in which to glory. But we can glory in Christ and the cross. On the cross, Christ broke everything that had us bound; we have been set free. Because of the cross and the resurrection the apostle Paul could write: "For he has rescued us from the dominion of darkness and brought us into the kingdom of the Son he loves" (Colossians 1:13).

Because of the resurrection, we not only have heaven to look forward to, but we have the power to live a new life today as we walk in relationship with our living Lord. Jesus is our hope for the future and our help for living in this present world. Through Him we can hold on when it seems there is nothing to hold on to. As we trust God and His Word, He daily renews our faith in Him. His mercies are new every morning. He brightens the daily path we walk.

In His own mysterious way, the Lord takes our unpleasant experiences and changes them for our good. Someone said, "He turns our 'bad' experiences into diamonds that will sparkle in our crown of life." Only with the blessings of the resurrection is such a feat possible!

15

The Living One Within Us

*How great is the love the Father has lavished on us,
that we should be called children of God! And that is
what we are! (1 John 3:1).*

When I was little girl, I always enjoyed wearing dresses my mother made for me. On Easter Sunday I especially looked forward to going to church wearing a new Easter dress. As a child, it seemed to me that Easter was a time to celebrate newness in every way possible. I still feel that way. That's why I particularly like these words from minister/author Jack Hayford: "No wonder so many people dress up in new clothes on Easter. It's just one more way to say, 'New life is here, and I'm celebrating the newness!' Jesus had new clothes on Easter, too."

What better reason for celebrating could anybody possibly think of? We're celebrating the resurrection and the new life we have in Jesus. Jesus has died and risen so that we might have life in Him. Not only will we have a future resurrection life, but we now have His resurrection life within us.

When troubles surround us, we can have hope. The Lord is always at work in our behalf. Because of Him, we can expect the unexpected. And Easter is the evidence that nothing is impossible with Him.

Quoting Jack Hayford again: "The very thought of the resurrection should fill the skies with our songs of triumph! Jesus has burst forth from the tomb and the open door of the grave shouts like a song-filled mouth— 'Christ is risen! Rejoice!'"

Having died and risen, Jesus lives forever, not only to forgive our sins, but to restore to us everything that the power of sin took away. He is our loving Savior and our victorious Lord. When the enemy comes against us to defeat or discourage us, we can rest in the assurance that there is One who is greater than he—and that powerful One lives within us.

One Easter Sunday several years ago in another town I attended a church service in which the pastor preached on the cross, graphically picturing all the horrible details of the crucifixion. No emphasis was given to the resurrection.

I went away not feeling at all as if it were Easter. Instead of celebrating Easter, we had been reminded of the awful price paid for our salvation. Maybe those who had no appreciation for the cross needed that reminder. But the Lord wants His children to *rejoice* on the day set aside for the celebration of His resurrection.

"There is something at the very center of our faith which reminds us that Good Friday may reign for a day," said Martin Luther King, Jr., "but ultimately it must give way to the triumphant beat of Easter drums."

Let's affirm with the psalmist:

> We will shout for joy . . . and will lift up
> our banners in the name of our God. . . . In
> him our hearts rejoice, for we trust in his
> holy name (Psalm 20:5; 33:21).

I am especially ready to join the psalmist in praise when I meditate on these words from Charles Stanley: "The powerful message of the resurrection is that God now inhabits the hearts of His people through the indwelling presence of His Holy Spirit. The next time you feel doubtful or discouraged, remember the power given to you by God through His Son. It is overcoming power from on high, and it is given to every person who places their trust in Jesus Christ."

Since Jesus by His Spirit actually lives in our mortal bodies, He imparts His divine life to us. We don't have to face life's struggles alone. We have His indwelling presence—His resurrection life and power. He is our help and our hope. We are no longer in darkness. Jesus said, "I have come into the world as a light, so that no one who believes in me should stay in darkness" (John 12:46).

Darkness is ignorance of divine truth, a lack of spiritual perception. Jesus came to be our light. His light is available to bring us enlightenment and eternal joy.

A. H. Ackley must have felt the joy of the Lord as he penned the words of the hymn we often sing at Easter:

I serve a risen Savior, He's in the world today;
I know that He is living, whatever men may say;
I see His hand of mercy, I hear His voice of cheer,
And just the time I need Him, He's always near.
He lives, He lives, Christ Jesus lives today!
He walks with me and talks with me
along life's narrow way.
He lives, He lives, salvation to impart!
You ask me how I know He lives?
He lives within my heart.

The knowledge and awareness that He lives within our hearts is sufficient to carry us through the daily routine of living. When things don't turn out the way we hoped they would, it's easy to forget that God is in charge. But the Holy Spirit is present to remind us—if we simply get still enough to listen.

We can celebrate Easter every day by remembering its purpose. Jesus came that we "may have life, and have it to the full" (John 10:10).

16

Fullness from Emptiness

The angel said to the women, "Do not be afraid, for I know that you are looking for Jesus, who was crucified. He is not here; he has risen, just as he said. Come and see the place where he lay" (Matthew 28:5,6).

The tombs of Egypt are famous because they contain the mummified bodies of ancient Egyptian kings. Westminster Abbey in London is renowned for containing bodies of English nobles. Mohammed's tomb is noted for its stone coffin with the bones of Mohammed.

But there is one tomb that is famous because it's empty—the garden tomb of Jesus. Imagine the alarm, the amazement, and the wonder that gripped the hearts of the women who found the tomb empty on that Easter morning! They had gone to anoint the body of Jesus.

As they approached the tomb, they suddenly realized that they would not be able to roll away the heavy stone. (The stone was a wheel of granite, eight feet in diameter and one foot thick, and weighing more than a ton.) But upon arriving there the women discovered that an angel had descended from heaven and rolled away the stone, and now sat on it.

I wonder if today some of us look for a dead Christ. That is, we fail to realize the significance of the resurrection. Christ died for us, and then rose for us—that we might be victorious in this life. It is important that we celebrate His resurrection and our new life in Him.

Michelangelo would agree. When he visited art galleries in Europe, he asked, "Why are art galleries filled with so many pictures of Christ upon the cross— Christ dying? Why do artists concentrate upon that as if it were the final scene? Christ is alive! He rules and triumphs."

Jesus says to you and me as the angel said to the fearful women at the tomb, "Do not be afraid. I am risen and alive." As Jesus was victorious over death, He lives and reigns to make us victorious in our daily lives. He invites us to turn our eyes upon Him and to trust Him to lead us through every circumstance.

Someone made the observation that the message we receive from the empty tomb depends upon who we are and what we are. Philosophers hear it and say, "Explain this event." Historians hear it and say, "Repeat this event." Time says, "Blot out this event." But we of faith hear the message of the empty tomb saying, "*Believe* this event."

An ancient legend tells of a monk who found the crown of thorns that Jesus wore. On Good Friday he set the cruel-looking crown on a side altar of the cathedral.

On Easter morning the monk entered the sanctuary to remove the crown of thorns. "This ugly reminder of Jesus' suffering would be out of place on Easter," he told himself. As he approached the altar, he detected an unusual fragrance. Coming nearer, he saw that the sun's rays had centered upon the crown. The warmth of the sun had changed the thorns into rare and beautiful roses with a sweet-smelling aroma.

That's only a story, of course. But when I read it, I thought of you and me. Our lives may be as unsightly as a twig of thorns. But the more we are exposed to the sunshine of the love of the resurrected Lord, the more like roses we become. And the fragrance of our lives blesses many other lives.

The apostle Paul expresses that thought in this way: "Thanks be to God, who always leads us in triumphal procession in Christ and through us spreads everywhere the fragrance of the knowledge of him. For we are to God the aroma of Christ among those who are being saved and those who are perishing," (2 Corinthians 2:14, 15).

Many years ago a German youth who had been taken prisoner by the Turks experienced the joy of the resurrection. He was forced to serve and live among the followers of Mohammed, but he never relinquished his faith in Christ. One Easter morning he was required to plow the field of a servant of Mohammed. As he worked, he sang an Easter hymn:

> Jesus Christ is risen,
> and o'er death triumphant reigns;
> leading sin herself in chains . . . .

At that moment an official of the German govern-ment rode by. Surprised to hear a religious hymn in that country, he stopped his carriage, approached the young man, and heard his story. "I don't ever expect to be able to return to my homeland," the youth conclud-ed, "but I shall preserve my Christian faith. And I'll always celebrate the resurrection."

The German official, impressed with the young man's testimony, obtained his freedom. The youth then went back to his homeland, where he celebrated future Easter Sundays with his family.

Our trials don't always have such a fortunate out-come, but our resurrected Lord is able to work His miracles in our hearts regardless of our circumstances.

Words
of
Vitality

17

Where Is My Focus?

The eyes of the LORD range throughout the earth to
strengthen those whose hearts are fully committed
to him (2 Chronicles 16:9).

Sitting in the waiting room of my orthopedic surgeon a few years ago, I noted a placard which could have been addressed directly to me. It read: "Attitudes are more important than facts." Then, as if to make sure I got the message, the same words pointed their fingers at me when I walked into the examining room a while later: "Attitudes are more important than facts."

The fact was that my wrist was not healing as rapidly as it should have. I was disappointed and discouraged. But my negative attitude could do nothing to change the facts. Such negative thinking could only hold me in bondage to a situation I had no power to change.

Too often I focus on the unpleasant things going on around me, instead of focusing on the Lord and letting Him handle the situation. I could take a lesson from the apostle Paul, who probably endured more hardships than any person in the New Testament. Paul said that regardless of what his circumstances might be, he had learned to be content.

This doesn't mean that Paul buried his head in the sand and ignored the facts. He looked beyond facts, knowing the truth he expressed in Romans 8:31: "If God is for us, who can be against us?" Paul knew that his life was committed to God and that God would not fail him. Sometimes it may look as if God has forgotten us, but He cannot. God always keeps His promises.

Paul had learned not to focus on his problems but on the Lord. In other words, Paul responded to the circumstances of life spiritually and not emotionally. Charles Stanley says, "If our daily decisions and actions are based on emotions, we will never be able to experience true spiritual contentment."

When our world turns upside down, our natural response is fretfulness and anxiety, and perhaps despair. We wonder how we can go on. We know that our sufficiency is in Christ, but when everything seems to be going wrong, we sometimes forget that the Lord is still on His throne and that He is aware of our needs.

The Lord wants to teach us contentment and complete trust in Him. We learn this truth (and most other important spiritual lessons) through difficult everyday experiences. If we never had to face difficulties, we would become self-sufficient. Our loving heavenly Father wants us to depend upon Him for all our needs, regardless of the nature of those needs.

Sometimes we have to be brought to the end of ourselves in order to be reminded of the Lord's provision.

When the doctor told me I would need physical therapy in order to restore the use of my hand, my first concern was having to spend hours every week in a clinic. I have other things I "need" to do, I complained to myself. Then my big concern became the high cost of receiving therapy. I could hardly believe the price quoted.

I realized I must get still before the Lord and let Him give me peace and direction. He reminded me again of His promise to supply. I turned to Jesus' teaching known as the Sermon on the Mount in Matthew's Gospel. Certain familiar phrases stood out:

> Do not worry about your life, what you will eat or drink; or about your body, what you will wear. . . . Look at the birds of the air; they do not sow or reap or store away in barns, and yet your heavenly Father feeds them. Are you not much more valuable than they? . . . So do not worry. . . . But seek first his kingdom and his righteousness, and all these things will be given to you as well (Matthew 6:25,26,31,33).

When our problems seem greater than the supply, we can remember that God has the solution. He knew from the beginning that all of us would face upsetting times in our lives. As you've probably heard someone say, "Life is not fair, but God is good." There is not a single situation in life that can defeat us if we look to Him in complete trust and confidence.

Over and over in His Word God reminds us of His goodness. We need to be constantly aware that God loves us with an unconditional love. He causes all things to work out for the good of us who belong to

Him. Our part is to trust Him and wait patiently. He uses shattering circumstances as a means of shaping us into the image of His Son and to make us more useful in His kingdom.

When we're tempted to doubt God's care, the best thing to do is to turn to His Word for reassurance. I have numerous Scriptures marked which I frequently read and meditate on. One of my favorites is 2 Thessalonians 3:16: "Now may the Lord of peace Himself grant you His peace [the peace of His kingdom] at all times and in all ways [under all circumstances and conditions, whatever comes]" (AMP).

David reminds us that God is always with us: "God is our refuge and strength, an ever-present help in trouble" (Psalm 46:1). When it seems that our personal world is giving way, that our strength is gone, and that all our hopes have fallen into the sea, God is our refuge.

God is never beyond our reach. He is not a far-off God who has to be searched for when we need Him. He is always present to comfort and encourage us. David tells us in Psalm 37:7, "Be still before the Lord and wait patiently for him." A hurried spirit keeps us from being aware of the Lord's presence. We all know how difficult it is to be aware of His presence when we're bothered about any situation. God knows this too. That's why He tells us to be still.

Many times the psalmist David had to flee for his life. He knew what it was to live in a shattered personal world. He said, "My soul finds rest in God alone" (Psalm 62:1). We may try to find rest or help in something or someone other than God, but God alone is our help.

We can do nothing on our own; we are helpless to help ourselves. But Christ lives in us by His Spirit and is within us to guide us and strengthen us when our world is shattered.

18

Children of the Most High

He has not despised or disdained the suffering
of the afflicted one; he has not hidden his face
from him but has listened to his cry for help
(Psalm 22:24).

Those who are rising above their troubled waters have learned to appropriate what they read in Scripture. They know, as the psalmist knew, that God "has listened to his cry for help." These people not only know about God, but they know Him in a meaningful, personal way.

They probably know that God's nature is revealed in His names. If you and I had lived in Old Testament times, we would know that God has many names, each name revealing a different aspect of His character. The names of God have many meanings which don't always come across in our English versions of the Bible.

One of God's most awesome names is *El Elyon*. Its usual translation is *God Most High*. We see it used in Psalm 91:1: "He who dwells in the shelter of the Most High will rest in the shadow of the Almighty."

When we dwell "in the shelter of the Most High," we recognize that God is far above all our problems and is able to strengthen us for them. He has the final word. He is all-powerful. When we accept God's invitation to dwell in His shelter, we are appropriating His blessings.

When we become anxious or worried, we move out from under His protective covering. Then we become vulnerable to the attacks of our spiritual enemy. We become prey for his darts.

The apostle Paul was one who knew how to appropriate the blessings of God and make them his own. Paul tells us that when God raised Christ from the dead, he "seated him at his right hand in the heavenly realms" and that God "raised us up with Christ and seated us with him in the heavenly realms in Christ Jesus" (Ephesians 1:20; 2:6).

That's too much for our finite minds to grasp. We wonder how we can be seated in the heavenly realms while living in our earthly bodies. But we can accept it by faith and know it's true because it's a part of the inspired Word of God.

Marilyn Hickey tells about a woman who got hold of that truth and won a victory over depression. Reading Paul's statement, she realized that if she was seated in heavenly places above all rule and satanic authority, she was above depression. She meditated on those Scriptures until they became a part of her very being. Eventually her depression lifted.

You and I are children of the Most High. His promises are ours. We can be transformed by His power.

19

He Knows and Cares

*Trust in the Lord with all your heart, and lean not on
your own understanding; in all your ways acknowledge
Him, and He shall direct your paths*
(Proverbs 3:5,6 NKJV).

One day I confessed to my pastor my discouragement over a certain situation. He suggested, "Go read one of the books you wrote!" I find myself constantly having to relearn the things I already know. I fail to take to heart the words of King Solomon to "lean not on your own understanding." I forget that God is in charge and I can trust Him to work everything out.

Several years ago I was on my way to a weeklong speaking engagement in another state when I broke a bone in my foot. Hurrying to change planes in a large airport, I turned my ankle and fell.

By the time I reached my destination that night my foot had swollen to almost twice its normal size. Still, I hoped I had only sprained my ankle. But the next morning I was in such pain that my hostess took me to her doctor in a small town. After examining the X-ray, the doctor concluded that I simply had a sprain. He did nothing for me. By the grace of God, I got through the week and continued to walk on that foot.

Several weeks later my foot was still hurting. I went to an orthopedic doctor in my own town. He took three X-rays and discovered I had a broken bone. For the next few weeks I walked with the aid of crutches.

The more knowledgeable physician saw what the other had failed to see. Many times others may not see or understand our needs. But the all-seeing eye of our Great Physician, Jesus Himself, sees and knows all about us. He knows every pain we feel. He not only sees and knows; He cares. No fracture (whether a bone or inner brokenness) is beyond His ability to detect and heal.

The good news is that we don't have to go on hurting. Properly cared for, broken bones eventually heal. Broken hearts can be healed by the love and power of our Father God. A friend recently wrote to me, "I'm living with almost unbearable stress. Why must a Christian continue to suffer emotional pain like I'm feeling?"

We are all affected by the sick society we live in. Our emotional pains often result from our messed-up world. We cannot change what people have done to us. But we *can* decide how *we* will respond.

If the Great Physician were to write a prescription for our stresses, it probably would include prayer, Bible reading, and meditation daily. He might advise us to combine the three, making them last 20 or 30 minutes per session. He probably would prescribe certain passages of Scripture for our meditation.

We can take the promises of God and make them ours, just as if they had our name on them. Solomon is saying in the verses quoted at the beginning of this chapter that we can cast ourselves fully on the Lord and expect Him to show us the way. Let's resist the temptation to brood over our situation. If we lean on the Lord, He will support us.

Peter says, "Casting the whole of your care [all your anxieties, all your worries, all your concerns, once and for all] on Him, for He cares for you affectionately and cares about you watchfully" (1 Peter 5:7 AMP).

Since we belong to God, He takes responsibility for us. He will protect us in every situation. All He asks is that we trust Him completely, letting Him do the work.

When we feel that we're lacking in faith, or that we're failures or weaklings, we might consider these words of Jack Hayford: "People of faith are weaklings who cast those weaknesses upon the shoulders of God and then stand firm in the servant-spirit of a true disciple; failures who put their failings under the blood of the Lamb and worship Him who is able to reconcile all things to Himself."

One trick of the enemy is to make us feel guilty for not being all we think we should be. We are sometimes tempted to believe we should be free of stress because we are Christians. But it is not so. We are human, and we live in a world of stressful situations. God understands that, and He understands us far better than we understand ourselves. He is more patient with us than we are with ourselves.

"The removal of stress is not automatic," says Charles Swindoll. "It is the cooperative effort of the Christian and his God. May our God be allowed entrance into your mind and be given the reins of your life so completely that all your stress is replaced with peace, as all your fear is removed by faith." This is my prayer for you and for me.

20

Uplift in Discouragement

You, O Lord, are a compassionate and gracious God,
slow to anger, abounding in love and faithfulness
(Psalm 86:15).

A discouraged man dreamed that he was standing on top of a granite rock, trying to break it with a pickax. After several hours of hard work with no results, he gave up. Suddenly a stranger appeared before him and asked, "Were you not assigned this task? If so, why are you not working at it?"

"I'm getting nowhere toward breaking the rock," the man replied. "I see no point in keeping on trying."

"That is not your assignment," the stranger said. "Your task is to pick whether the rock yields or not. The work is yours. The results are in other hands. Keep working."

How many times have you felt like quitting when you saw no results from your efforts? How easy it is to become discouraged when nothing seems to be happening! We forget that the results are not our responsibility, but God's.

"Probably nothing else bothers sincere Christians as much as those dry spells that come from time to time," says Michael Horban, a pastor in Ontario, Canada. "They come no matter how earnestly one tries to please God. There are days, even weeks, when we trudge through discouragement."

We cannot read the Scriptures without noticing that many great men and women of Bible times became discouraged. Imagine how despondent Hagar must have felt when cast out of Abraham's household. How discouraged the Israelites were while under the cruel oppression of the Egyptians. Could Moses have been anything less than discouraged many times while on his mission to lead the Israelites out of Egypt? What about David, Job, Elijah, Jonah, and Jeremiah?

So when we're discouraged, let's remember that our experience is not unusual. It might also be well to ask ourselves if we're trying to do more than God is asking us to do. Are we struggling over something we have no control over? The Christian life was never meant to be a frustrating struggle. But we sometimes make it one, and then allow discouragement to overtake us.

God understands our feelings of discouragement and the reason for those feelings. He never condemns us for the way we feel. "For God did not send his Son into the world to condemn the world" (John 3:17). Eventually our spiritual spring will flow again, but we need not condemn ourselves if it doesn't flow as soon as we had hoped.

Faith is not dependent on feelings. We can refuse the enemy's lies when he tells us we're guilty for feeling as we do. Our faith rests in the unshakable character of God. He looks at our heart, our motives, our desires, and our obedience to Him. He declares that we're still valuable to Him. He will lift us up. "No pit is so deep that He is not deeper still," says Charles Swindoll in his book *Encourage Me*. "No valley so dark that the light of His truth cannot penetrate."

In times of discouragement, it often helps to lose ourselves in an inspirational book. I've done that many times. Good books feed my soul when nothing else can. God not only uses His Holy Word to speak to us, but also the inspirational writings of others.

There have been times when I could only go to the Lord and pour out my heart to Him. If in my discouragement I *felt* that God was far away, I nevertheless *knew* that He was near. I had to learn not to rely on my own feelings, but upon the reality that God will never leave me nor forsake me.

I'm sure the psalmist did that many times. On one occasion he cried, "In you, O LORD, I have taken refuge; ... Turn your ear to me, come quickly to my rescue; be my rock of refuge, a strong fortress to save me" (Psalm 31:1,2).

The same consolation that so often brought joy to David's soul can bring joy to our own souls. We need only to quiet ourselves in God's presence. If we're unable to hear Him speak in our spirit, we can let Him speak to us through the Psalms. We know that the promises that were David's are for us too. We might pray this prayer of David's:

You are forgiving and good, O Lord, abounding in love to all who call to you. Hear my prayer, LORD; listen to my cry for mercy. In the day of my trouble I will call to you, for you will answer me (Psalm 86:5-7).

We cannot always be sure of what will happen in our lives, but we can always be sure of God's love and faithfulness. That's what counts, especially when we feel discouraged.

Words
of
Commitment

21

Eyes to See God

How precious to me are your thoughts, O God! How vast is the sum of them! (Psalm 139:17).

Augustine was once approached by a heathen who showed him his idol and said, "Here is my god. Where is yours?" Augustine replied, "I can't show you my God, not because He doesn't exist but because you have no eyes to see Him."

You and I have eyes to see God. But I sometimes wonder if our spiritual vision is so impaired that we are far from seeing Him as He really is. Is our view of God so limited that we fail to realize that He is a God of unconditional love and that He is completely committed to us?

We do not earn God's love. There's nothing we can say or do that will make Him love us any more than He already does. We are not loved more because of anything we do. Rather, we are able to do what we do *because* of His love for us. "Measuring up" is not part of God's requirement for love. He loves us simply because we belong to Him.

Minister/author Lloyd Ogilvie says when he gets exhausted, the Savior is waiting with an offer: "Take off that yoke. Here, join me in mine. I'll take the burden of your need." If we listen, we might hear Him say that or similar words to us. That's the kind of God we serve.

J. B. Phillips says in his book *Your God Is Too Small* that the trouble with many people today is that the God they know is too small for their modern needs. He explains that while our experiences of life have expanded, we have clung to childhood ideas of God. Maybe we see Him as a Santa Claus who rewards us when we're good and neglects us when we're bad.

I have a Christian friend who obviously knows that kind of God. She wonders if God is displeased with her behavior when it's perfectly normal. She's afraid to accept her own humanness. Her conscience works overtime, keeping her in misery much of the time. She can't live up to her own standards of perfection. Then she projects her judgment of herself onto God, and doubts whether God loves her.

God is a God of love, compassion, and forgiveness, not a God of wrath. His wrath is poured out only on those who deliberately rebel against Him. If you read the Old Testament and neglect the New, you might conclude that God is a vengeful God. But His vengefulness was against those who refused to obey Him, never against His own children.

Jesus came to show us what the Father is like. He said, "Anyone who has seen me has seen the Father" (John 14:9). The writer to the Hebrews tells us, "The Son is the radiance of God's glory and the exact representation of his being" (Hebrews 1:3). When we look at the compassionate words and works of Jesus, we see the Father's likeness.

Jesus spoke and did only what He saw the Father doing and saying. He declared, "I tell you the truth, the Son can do nothing by himself; he can do only what he sees his Father doing, because whatever the Father does the Son also does" (John 5:19).

The psalmist David knew God as few others have known Him. He said, "I praise you because I am fearfully and wonderfully made; your works are wonderful, I know that full well" (Psalm 139:14). How difficult it is for us to believe that God has made us wonderfully! Our loving God places more value on us as His children than we place on ourselves.

Then why do things happen that seem to be strongly against us? Because of the fall of the human race. We're all under the influence of Adam's fall. But the God who promises to see us through every trial and circumstance will not let us down. When our will is aligned with His, we can expect His blessings. We may have to wait longer than we think we should, but our God will not fail us.

Various kinds of distresses are natural in the life of all Christians. But we can rejoice, knowing that God provides us with supernatural grace.

I had a friend who was a perfect example of someone who knew how to rejoice in the Lord and rest in His grace. She has gone to her eternal home. During her last several months on earth she suffered such intense pain that she wore a morphine pump inside her body. But through it all she never complained. She continually rejoiced in the Lord, whom she recognized as a big God. She never doubted God's goodness or His commitment to her.

My friend would say with Paul, "We also rejoice in our sufferings, because we know that suffering produces perseverance; perseverance, character; and character, hope. And hope does not disappoint us, because God has poured out his love into our hearts by the Holy Spirit, whom he has given us" (Romans 5:3-5).

Maybe my friend was a little like the sailor in a shipwreck who was thrown upon a rock, where he clung in great danger until the tide went down. Later someone asked him, "Didn't you shake with fear when you were clinging to that rock?" He replied, "Yes, but the rock didn't."

You and I may shake with fear many times in this life, but we have a big God. He is our unshakable Rock to whom we can safely cling. He will never go back on His commitment to us!

22

God Will Not Fail Us

I tell you, do not worry about your life, what you will eat or drink; or about your body, what you will wear. Is not life more important than food, and the body more important than clothes? (Matthew 6:25).

What's going to happen to us? Everything is changing for the worse. I'm worried," says a friend.

Have you heard similar concerns? To say to others during trying times, "Simply trust the Lord," may sound pious. Yet we know that God is committed to us and will not fail us. This morning I read again the story of Moses and the plagues that God sent upon Egypt before Pharaoh let the Israelites go free. None of the plagues affected God's people. He protected His own and provided for them. He also cares that much for us (Exodus chapters 7-12).

When we worry instead of trusting God, we open the door to fear. Jesus knew we would face temptations to doubt His care. That's why He told His disciples in the Sermon on the Mount, "Look at the birds of the air; they do not sow or reap or store away in barns, and yet your heavenly Father feeds them. Are you not much more valuable than they?" (Matthew 6:26).

Our problem is that we've read such verses for years, looked at them through our tinted traditional glasses, and failed to grasp their truth. We seem not to realize that Jesus' words are as much for today as when He spoke them.

I gain encouragement by rereading certain Scriptures to refresh my memory that God is my supply. It's when I take my eyes off God and His promises and focus on circumstances that I become overly concerned. You and I are in covenant relationship with God. God lovingly chose to enter into this relationship with us, and nothing can break that covenant.

The Lord proclaims Himself to be "the LORD, the compassionate and gracious God, slow to anger, abounding in love and faithfulness" (Exodus 34:6). God's love, nature, and power never change.

In the words of Charles Stanley, "When God thinks of you, He envisions you living freely and joyfully within His love and grace." If I could always see myself as God sees me—in His love and grace, protected and provided for—I would never worry about my future. I would remember that the same God who provided manna for the Israelites in the desert can do the same for me if necessary. Isaiah reminds us, "The LORD longs to be gracious to you; he rises to show you compassion . . . . Blessed are all who wait for him!" (Isaiah 30:18).

Pastor Jack Hayford reminds us, "You and I need the Lord's help every second, every minute, every day. Acknowledging our honest dependency is not resigning our own responsibilities, but it is the most logical stance a creature can take. We have been made by Him and we must be sustained by Him."

Another help in facing the future unafraid is, of course, prayer. Even though we read God's promises in His Word, we are to *ask* for them. Asking implies trust. Our trust flows out of our understanding of who God is and our relationship to Him.

If we believe that the Lord really is God and that we are His, isn't it strange that we so often fail to come to Him in confidence that He will hear and answer us? Fear and nervous tension melt away when we are aware of the loving presence of the Lord.

I heard a song by an unknown author a few months ago which has especially blessed me. I hope you will be blessed by the words as I was.

Lay your burden down,
Put your cares away.
Place your eyes on Him,
He will lead your way.
He'll always be with you
Until the end of your day.
Be still and know that I am God.

23

His Life Through Us

*I delight in weaknesses. . . . For when I am weak, then
I am strong (2 Corinthians 12:10).*

I have a friend who is helplessly struggling to
"be good." Since she thinks she's failing, she
feels that God cannot love her. She has
overlooked the promise that nothing can separate her
from God's love (Romans 8:39). She hasn't realized
that our Christian life is *Christ living His life in us*.

We may feel that we have to imitate the life of Christ
in order to please Him. The fact is that He desires to live
His life *through* us. After our new birth, our real self is
Christ living in us. There's no struggle. Paul says, "He who
unites himself with the Lord is one with him in spirit"
(1 Corinthians 6:17). Regardless of our feelings, the fact
is that we are one with the Spirit of Christ.

Again, Paul explains it clearly: "I have been crucified
with Christ and I no longer live, but Christ lives in me.
The life I live in the body, I live by faith in the Son of
God, who loved me and gave himself for me"
(Galatians 2:20).

As Malcolm Smith puts it, "The Christian life is not trying to practice some cold set of principles of Christianity, but actually knowing Christ lives through me.... Wherever you go, whatever you may feel, Christ is within you, motivating you and living His life in yours."

The adversary is only too eager to plant doubts in our minds and make us question our standing with God. He puts thoughts in our minds and makes us think they are *our* thoughts. Satan discourages us and makes us feel unworthy. We may need to remind ourselves often of who we are in Christ:

> *We're the people of God,*
> *Called by His name,*
> *Called from the dark,*
> *And delivered from shame.*
>
> —Author unknown

We no longer need to struggle under the law. The law simply showed us our condition without Christ. It was given to show us our helplessness to save ourselves. Christ fulfilled the law for us. We can do nothing to earn God's favor. We are helpless receivers of His free grace. P. P. Bliss expressed it in these words of his hymn "Once for All":

> *Free from the law, O happy condition,*
> *Jesus has bled, and there is remission;*
> *Cursed by the law and bruised by the fall,*
> *Grace has redeemed us, once for all.*

A new Christian may fret because in many ways he feels no different from the way he felt before he accepted Christ. The pressures of life cause him to feel worried or angry, and he feels guilty for those feelings. It may take time for such feelings to change. When autumn comes, it takes time for all the leaves to fall off a tree.

The pressures of life are opportunities for us to let Christ live in us. When we feel weak and helpless, we can remember Paul's words and know they can apply to us: "I delight in weaknesses. . . . For when I am weak, then I am strong."

Quoting Malcolm Smith, "The law will constantly confront you saying its 'oughts' and 'shoulds.' . . . Smile and thank God that you have come to death concerning your natural ability. Your life is no longer a straitjacket of rules, but the life of Christ lived through your weakness. . . . His love is an infinitely wise love that not only forgives but actually weaves our mistakes into His plans and turns them into good."

That sounds too good to be true. But wouldn't we say that all of the gospel sounds too good to be true? When we give our lives to Christ, He makes something beautiful of them, whether we feel that way or not.

Sometimes we make the mistake of comparing ourselves with other people, and then condemning ourselves for not being like them. But we don't know what they had to go through in order to arrive at the place where we see them.

For instance, we look at the life of the great man of faith, George Mueller, and we wish we had such faith.

The writer of his biography says, "The building of Mr. Mueller's spiritual life was a constant conflict. While outwardly he displayed a calm attitude, inwardly he battled to obtain this seeming peace."

Mr. Mueller wrote, "Think not that I have the gift of faith. If I were only one moment left by myself, my faith would utterly fail." Mueller's "victories came through prayer, trust in the Lord's unfailing promises and faith that God's truth could not fail." It was the testing of his faith that drove George Mueller to prayer and great faith.

God makes no two of us alike. He knows what is necessary to bring us to the place where He wants us to be. But it's His doing, not ours.

God's desire is to live His life in and through us. Oswald Chambers says God's purpose in getting us where He wants us to be is "that we may realize all that identification with Jesus means." It's a life of rest in Him! That's a part of God's commitment to us.

24

True Rejoicing

*The LORD your God is with you, he is mighty to save. He
will take great delight in you, he will quiet you with his love,
he will rejoice over you with singing
(Zephaniah 3:17).*

*D*o you ever feel that every time you read
your Bible the same thought jumps out at
you? When that happens repeatedly, the
Lord is saying, "Pay attention to this." For a period of
time the subject for me was joy. The Lord wanted me
to know His joy and that He rejoices over me. He
wants us all to know that His commitment to love us
includes His rejoicing over us.

"Joy means the perfect fulfillment of that for which
I was created and regenerated, not the successful doing
of a thing," says Oswald Chambers. When we live in
conscious union with the Lord, we rest *joyfully* in Him.
We rejoice in the knowledge of His indwelling presence. We take time to smell the fragrance of His creation. And we take time to enjoy the Lord and the
knowledge of His commitment to us.

Before Jesus left this earth in bodily form, He taught His disciples many truths which are recorded in His Word. Among other things, He wanted to make sure His disciples understood His desire for His joy to live on in them. He said, "I have told you this so that my joy may be in you and that your joy may be complete" (John 15:11).

What was the joy of Jesus? Where did it come from? Jesus found joy and fulfillment in doing the will of the Father. As Jesus trusted the Father to lead Him in all He did, we can expect Him to do the same for us. We can trust Him to lead us hour by hour and day by day, even in our mundane daily chores. In the midst of our work, we can have joyful communion with our Lord.

The Lord is waiting to heal our inner hurts which keep us from experiencing His love and joy at a deep level. Our understanding of the depth of God's love and commitment to us continues as long as we live.

Some of us who are on "a journey of discovery" of deeper joy and growth face the challenge of being patient with ourselves. God is patient with us and desires that we be patient with ourselves. When we accept ourselves as we are, we are better able to be convinced of God's commitment to us in every area of our need.

25

Accepted in Christ

May your whole spirit, soul and body be kept blameless
at the coming of our Lord Jesus Christ
(1 Thessalonians 5:23).

Have you ever watched a butterfly flit from flower to flower or a sparrow hop from branch to branch and wished you were that free—free from care or worry? You and I are too often weighted down with care. Our cares exist because of pressures of today or hurts from the past, or because we are sorrowful or unhappy for some reason.

Too many of us have never felt sufficient love and acceptance. We would do well to hear the truth spoken by G. K. Chesterton: "All men matter. You matter. I matter. It's the hardest thing in theology to believe." Most of us have received too many put-downs and heard too many legalisms to believe that we really matter. In God's eyes we matter significantly.

Until we know that we matter to God and to others, we doubt our value in His sight. We don't realize that we have a unique, God-given purpose in life. And even if we know that, we may not know how to arrive at the place we'd like to be, spiritually and emotionally. We may wonder whether we're being true to our real selves. We often try to do more than we should.

With so many voices in the world and so many demands on our time, it's easy to get our priorities out of order. I've always been an avid reader. I have hundreds of books in my personal library, and I'm still buying books. My problem is that too often I try to imitate those I read about and admire. But God has not asked me to imitate others. He wants me to be the person He created *me* to be, true to the desires He placed in *my* heart.

Sometimes we are so intent on pleasing others or doing what others think we ought to do that we neglect the person closest to us—ourselves. It is possible to be so busy in church that we fail to do the two most important things—develop our own inner life and maintain intimacy with God.

In his newsletter, Joseph Girzone aptly says, "The healing we all need can only come from a warm, personal contact with Jesus and an intimate understanding of how He feels about us." Taken by themselves, neither theology nor the church can bring the spiritual and emotional healing we need. It comes from grasping the depth of God's love and His commitment to us.

We all need healing reinforcement. You have read Augustine's statement to God: "You have made us for yourself, and our souls find no rest until they find it in you." We know that, and we try to arrive at that place of rest.

Perhaps the reason some people doubt their salvation is that they expect to be perfect. But only Jesus was perfect. He wants us to be patient while He works within us. "The one who calls you is faithful and he will do it" (1 Thessalonians 5:24).

In the words of Jack Hayford, "Rebirth, redemption, restoration and recovery are only part of His mission. He wants to bring you to full realization as well; the realization of God's purposes, patterns and promises for your life."

Meanwhile we are to rejoice in Him, trusting Him (in His time) to do what is needed to bring us to the place of feeling as free as the birds and butterflies appear to be.

26

The Blessedness of Waiting

The steps of a good man are ordered by the LORD,
and He delights in his way
(Psalm 37:23 NKJV).

Several years ago when I was in the hospital, a young man was brought into the room next to mine. He kept crying out, "Why doesn't the doctor come in? I need him now."

No one likes to wait. Yet it seems that life is liberally punctuated with periods of waiting. Waiting at red lights. Waiting for a long-hoped-for letter. Waiting for circumstances to change. Waiting for the nurse to call us from the waiting room.

Perhaps the most common and most frustrating period of waiting is that of waiting for prayer to be answered. Like the young man in the hospital room, we cry out, "Why does God keep me waiting? I need an answer now."

That great man of prayer, Andrew Murray, said, "Be assured that if God waits longer than you could wish, it is only to make the blessing doubly precious. God waited four thousand years, till the fullness of time, ere He sent His Son. Our times are in His hands; He will avenge His elect speedily; He will make haste for our help, and not delay one hour too long."

We have difficulty remembering that our times and our lives are in God's hands, no matter what. We think we know what is best, and we wonder why God doesn't answer in the way and in the time we think He should. We are prone to start wondering if we misunderstood God's promise, or if something is wrong with our lives, when in reality we are walking as closely to Him and as dedicatedly as we know how.

A man came upon the great New England preacher Phillips Brooks, who was usually calm and collected, and saw him pacing the floor. "What's the trouble, Dr. Brooks?" asked the friend. Brooks replied, "The trouble is that I'm in a hurry, but God isn't!"

Sometimes we wait for what seems to us like an extremely long time, but no answer comes. And in fact the answer may never come in the way we expect. But we can be sure it will come in the way God knows is best for us. Again and again I have to remind myself that God is in charge of my life and that He always knows best. He is committed to doing what is best for me at all times.

A friend of George Mueller told of being alone in Mr. Mueller's study. Thinking it would be a good time to look at the Bible of this man of faith and achievement, he opened it and thumbed through it. He came to an underlined verse— "The steps of a good man are ordered by the LORD" (Psalm 37:23 KJV). Mueller had written in the margin, "And the *stops* too."

How unlike most of us! We think we must keep moving, keep being productive. If we get stopped in our efforts, we start looking to see what we've done wrong or how we can make up for lost time. It may be that the Lord allowed the stop in order to get our attention focused on Him.

Dr. Charles Stanley often reminds us in his little *In Touch* magazine that God's greatest desire for His people is that we have a close personal relationship with Him. "God doesn't *need* any of us to fulfill His role as God," says Dr. Stanley, "but what He does desire is our worship, praise and adoration. He longs for us to call out to Him and to desire Him above anyone and anything." Sometimes that comes about best during our forced *waiting* times.

We look at waiting times as trials, but we might do better to view them as opportunities—opportunities for God to speak and to make Himself more real to us, opportunities simply to rest in Him.

Oswald Chambers says, "There are not three stages in spiritual life—worship, waiting and work. Some of us go in jumps like spiritual frogs. We jump from worship to waiting, and from waiting to work. God's idea is that the three should go together. . . . It is a discipline, and we cannot get into it all at once."

Words
of
Comfort

27

Real Prayer

No matter how many promises God has made, they are
"Yes" in Christ. And so through him the "Amen" is
spoken by us to the glory of God
(2 Corinthians 1:20).

O ne day I knelt beside my bed and "prayed,"
but nothing happened. I felt no change, no
peace of mind. On another occasion I had
hardly begun to pray when I sensed a still voice saying,
"I want this more than you do, so you can rest in the
assurance that it's done."

What made the difference? In the first instance, I
hadn't really prayed. I had already made up my mind
about what I wanted, without first asking for God's will
in the matter. In the next instance, I knew God's will
and asked for it to be done. My sincere prayer was
answered. We may not always know God's will, but
that doesn't keep us from praying. God understands
our frailties. He honors our motives.

Real prayer begins in the mind of God. He prompts
us to pray for certain people and circumstances. He

uses us to accomplish His will on earth through prayer.

God wants to fulfill His promises, but He often waits for us to ask for them to be fulfilled. God has given us the privilege of becoming colaborers with Him to bring about His will on earth.

God does not want us to pray "in the dark." His desire is to reveal His will to us. Of course, we are weak and there are times when we are not sure of the will of God. But often we need only to look in His Word and listen to His Spirit to find His will. The better we know Him and His Word, the more we can be sure of His will.

Bible teacher Pat Robertson cautions us, "Be careful not to start or end a prayer by saying blindly, 'If it be your will.' Rather you should seek to know God's will in the situation and then base your prayer upon it."

Prayer is much more than merely saying words. It may be that some of our best praying is done in silence. Prayer is first of all a relationship with our heavenly Father. It is being aware of God's presence. In his book *Prayer*, O. Hallesby says, "Prayer is an attitude of the heart. . . . Whether it takes the form of words or not does not mean anything to God, only to ourselves."

Prayers don't have to be long. We don't need to use King James English (thee and thou, etc.). Neither does prayer necessarily follow a formula. Prayer is talking to God. It can be as natural and easy as talking to our best friend.

God never asks us to come to Him with our strengths. He doesn't ask us to make ourselves worthy. He wants to assure us that we have been made worthy through Christ. Sometimes we may feel that God is far away or that our prayers are not heard. That could be a suggestion from the enemy. We are in a spiritual battle and must be on guard for Satan's schemes. He will do everything in his power to keep us from praying and to make us feel that God is not present with us.

In addition to a scheduled time of prayer each day, we can call upon God at any time and know that He is there. "Learn how to pray in the streets or in the country," said Thomas Merton. "Know how to meditate not only when you have a book in your hand but when you are waiting for a bus or riding on a train." We might add, "Know how to pray when you're in the shower, or dressing for the day, or washing dishes, or whatever you might be doing."

Have you noticed how the psalmists expressed so honestly their feelings to God? Their emotions raced up and down, just as ours do. The psalmists made no effort to hide their feelings, whether good or bad. On one occasion David cried out to God, "Why are You so far from helping me?" Of course God is never far away from any of us. But He understands our feelings and is never upset with us.

Jim Auer says, "A good parent isn't upset with a toddler who falls and "fails" many times in learning to walk. . . . God is your perfect parent, who knows perfectly well that your falls and fumblings in prayer are simply steps in your progress toward deeper union with God." Isn't that a comforting thought?

28

Not Bitter But Better

*The LORD is my light and my salvation—whom shall
I fear? The LORD is the stronghold of my life—of
whom shall I be afraid? (Psalm 27:1).*

Of the many persons who could have been
bitter about life, the black slave George
Washington Carver was one of them. His
father died before his birth. The young boy got sepa-
rated from his mother when he and she were abducted
from the Carver farm. He never saw his mother again.

Nothing in history indicates that any bitterness
ever sprang up in George. At the age of ten he accepted Christ as his Savior. You may know his story:
Overcoming the odds against him—poverty and slav-
ery—he eventually graduated from college and became
the great Christian man we know him to have been. In
spite of hardships and racial prejudice against him,
Carver refused to be bitter.

A biblical example of a person who could have been
bitter but chose blessing instead is Hannah. Hannah

was one of the two wives of Elkanah. The other wife, Peninnah, constantly scoffed at Hannah and made life miserable for her because Hannah had no children. Year after year, Hannah wept and longed for a son while her rival continued to provoke her.

But instead of becoming bitter, Hannah went to the temple and prayed. "And she made a vow, saying, 'O LORD Almighty, if you will only look upon your servant's misery and remember me, and not forget your servant but give her a son, then I will give him to the LORD for all the days of his life'" (1 Samuel 1:11). From that day until her son was born, Hannah went about comforted and full of joy, knowing that her prayer had been heard. Her faith rewarded her with blessing—the birth of Samuel.

Life on this earth is filled with opportunities for bitterness. Circumstances in life seem terribly unfair for many of us. Parents disappoint their children. Children disappoint their parents. Friends or loved ones misunderstand us. Health problems arise. Financial difficulties emerge unexpectedly. A loved one passes away. Hopes are dashed. Blessings are postponed.

We have the option of becoming bitter or of releasing our problems to the Lord and receiving the blessing of His comfort. If we follow the pattern of the world, we will become bitter. That's the easy but destructive route. That's the path which our adversary, the devil, has chosen for us. He delights not only in making us bitter but also in discouraging us. The devil honors no boundaries except those we choose to set by our faith, prayer, and obedience to God's Word.

God's intent has never been for His people to become bitter over any circumstance, but to trust Him for eventual blessing. God never creates our problems, but He is with us in them. He is bigger than our problems. Trusting God brings us to the place of joy in the midst of circumstances which would make non-Christians bitter. Only as we look beyond our circumstances to God can we receive His comfort. Only then can we receive the blessing He means for us.

In his foreword to the book, *Gold in the Making*, Lloyd Ogilvie says, "Pain, suffering, and trouble are a part of life. There's no escape. God does not send it, but He uses it to refine us into the great people He intended us to be. Suffering will make or break us." Trouble can make us bitter, or it can be turned into a blessing, depending on how we respond.

What we must remember when trials and disappointments come is that God still loves us totally and unconditionally. He never takes His eyes off His children. He is not watching to see if we're "behaving ourselves," but instead is watching to protect us. He won't let the fire become too hot for us to bear.

Our loving Father knows that we're human. He never condemns us for being tempted to become fearful or bitter. He simply reminds us that He is present to deliver us from those negative attitudes and to bless us with His comfort and peace.

In his book *Chosen for Blessing*, Norman Wright titles his first chapter "Born to Be Blessed." I wonder if that is not exactly opposite of the way many people feel about themselves today. Yet when we consider the

Scriptures, we realize it's true: God has chosen to bless us in Christ.

Old as well as New Testament writers knew that God was committed to blessing them. In the midst of circumstances which might have made most others bitter, the psalmist made such declarations as, "Surely goodness and mercy will follow me all the days of my life" (Psalm 23:6 KJV).

The Lord said through Jeremiah, "I will make an everlasting covenant with them: I will never stop doing good to them" (Jeremiah 32:40). Those same promises are ours. The Lord delights in blessing and comforting us in our times of need.

29

The Life of Trust

Do not fear, for I am with you; do not be dismayed,
for I am your God. I will strengthen you and help you;
I will uphold you with my righteous right hand
(Isaiah 41:10).

When a mother giraffe's offspring comes into the world, the first thing the mother does is to hurl her newborn into the air. She watches while it falls to the ground. She waits a minute and gives it a kick. If the calf is slow to respond, she repeats her action. When the calf finally stands up for the first time on its wobbly legs, its mother kicks it off its feet.

Sounds cruel, doesn't it? But the mother giraffe is teaching her baby how to respond quickly. She instinctively knows that in order to survive, a young giraffe must be able to get up quickly so it can stay with the herd. Only then is it safe from its enemies.

Do you sometimes feel as if you've just got back on your feet from a trial when you get knocked down by another problem? As the kicks received by the baby

124

giraffe prepare it for survival, the knockdowns we receive prepare us for a life of trust. Our one consolation is that God knows and cares. God *never causes* our problems or pains. But He is aware of what is going on in our lives and works out everything for our good.

God wants to us to be prepared for what lies ahead. He reminds us over and over in His Word to trust Him and not be anxious. Many of the Psalms tell us to rejoice in the Lord. We are not told to rejoice because of what's happening. We rejoice simply because we know God loves us. In times of trial, rejoicing calls for faith and the realization that God is still on His throne.

God knows what the end will be: "We know that in all things God works for the good of those who love him, who have been called according to his purpose" (Romans 8:28). You may have heard people ask, "Where is God when I'm going through all this?" God understands our need for questions, and He doesn't mind our asking. However, He often chooses not to answer. He seems to say, "Simply trust me and wait. I will use your trials."

We can look at the lives of those in past generations who have experienced misfortune and note how God used their trials to make them a blessing to others. For instance, remember the story of Helen Keller, who became blind and deaf in early childhood? After she learned to speak, she inspired thousands with her messages of faith. Once she said, "The world is full of the overcoming of troubles."

Many of the old hymns we sing were inspired by aching hearts. I don't know what inspired George Mathiason to write "O Love That Wilt Not Let Me Go," but many people have discovered deep meaning in his words in the midst of their heartaches. Let's look at the first stanza.

> O love that wilt not let me go,
> I rest my weary soul in Thee;
> I give Thee back the life I owe,
> That in Thine ocean depths its flow
> May richer, fuller be.

Another hymnwriter with whose songs we are familiar was the blind Fanny J. Crosby. If she had not been blind, she might not have been the great hymnwriter we know her to have been. One of her lessknown hymns is one you may find encouraging if you're tired waiting for God to lead you out of the darkness:

> Child of God, wait patiently,
> When dark thy path may be;
> And let thy faith lean trustingly
> On Him who cares for thee;
> And though the clouds hang drearily
> Upon the brow of night,
> Yet in the morning joy will come
> And fill thy soul with light!

In his book *Turn It to Gold*, James Kennedy says, "I think it is safe to say that every life is shaped, to a large extent, by what it does with the troubles it experiences ....The way we respond, the way we either open ourselves to God's grace or close our hearts to it, determines the degree to which we allow God to take our troubles and turn them to gold."

A little later, Dr. Kennedy says troubles clear the way for a greater work of God. I've found that to be true in my life. I would not now change the circumstances that I would like to have escaped while they were happening. The troubles which felt so unbearable at the time prepared me for a much more fulfilling life than I could have known without them. God not only became more real to me, but He made it possible for me to help others to see more clearly how real He is.

I have always loved and appreciated the Word of God, but many of the Scriptures took on new life for me when I found no other place to turn for help. I often "lost" myself in my Bible, especially in certain Psalms and the book of Isaiah, beginning with chapter 40. I underlined many verses to make them easy to find for future reference and meditation.

I realize that the trials of each of us are different. But our feelings about them are similar: We want our troubles to hurry and end. The dark tunnel seems endless, but how brightly the sun shines when we finally emerge from the tunnel! We may need to remind ourselves often that God knows and that He has not deserted us. He is the God of all comfort.

30

Prepared for the Battle

Be self-controlled and alert. Your enemy the devil
prowls around like a roaring lion looking for someone to
devour. Resist him, standing firm in the faith
(1 Peter 5:8,9).

When the Civil War began, the North was totally unprepared for battle. Strange as it may seem, crowds of civilians followed the troops to the first battle, carrying picnic baskets, expecting to see a speedy victory. Soldiers arrived at the front not wearing their army gear because the armor was cumbersome. Of course, the North lost the first battle. They were not prepared.

Some of us think of spiritual warfare in the same way. We don't understand the importance of putting on the full armor of God as outlined in Ephesians 6:11-18. We are not prepared for spiritual battle unless we wear our armor continually.

Years were spent in study before man first set foot on the moon. The astronauts knew in advance that they would be in a different kind of environment. They wore special suits to provide oxygen. The utmost care was taken to ensure survival.

Unfortunately, our increased knowledge of the physical universe has not increased our sense of the spiritual. Too many Christians fail to realize the kind of spiritual environment we are in. In order to function successfully in the spiritual world, we need to know certain facts about the invisible realm of which we are a part.

We are not to be consumed with fear or have our minds overly occupied with thoughts of our spiritual adversary. However, to walk in spiritual victory we must be aware of the enemy's tactics.

We must take a stand against the devil's schemes, putting on the armor of God. Paul says, "Stand firm then, with the belt of truth buckled around your waist, with the breastplate of righteousness in place" (Ephesians 6:14). Unless we have a firm grasp of the truth of God's Word, we will be easy targets for the enemy.

Someone suggested that the belt of truth is what holds the rest of the armor in place. We can be comforted in knowing that our breastplate of righteousness is in place, because we are righteous through Christ. Reminding ourselves of that fact can help us to live in righteousness. Tyndale's commentary says that to neglect righteousness is to leave a gaping hole in our armor. With the breastplate in place, we can rely confidently on God instead of looking introspectively at ourselves.

Next, Paul says, stand "with your feet fitted with the readiness that comes from the gospel of peace" (verse 15). Peace is a state of inner rest. Now that we have the peace of God in our hearts, we are prepared to take that peace to others, whether it be by living in a state of forgiveness or by whatever means the Lord may suggest.

Next comes the shield of faith, "with which you can extinguish all the flaming arrows of the evil one" (verse 16). The shield of faith protects us against the doubts which the enemy places in our path. We can never base our faith upon our own strengths, but when our faith is in God, He gives us the power to overcome the enemy's assaults. Focusing our attention on God and not on our weaknesses enables us to face our circumstances courageously. We may not *feel* courageous, but we live by faith, not feelings.

Lastly Paul says, "Take the helmet of salvation and the sword of the Spirit, which is the word of God" (verse 17). Salvation refers to the complete redemptive process, which includes the renewing of our minds by Bible reading and prayer.

The sword of the Spirit—the Word of God—is our primary weapon. Our use of this weapon not only defeats the enemy but comforts and strengthens us. The psalmist said to the Lord, "I have hidden your word in my heart that I might not sin against you" (Psalm 119:11).

Paul does not describe prayer as a part of the armor, but he mentions it in the same verse in which he mentions the helmet of salvation. Our weaponry is incomplete without prayer. We put on each part of the armor with prayer.

Paul concludes his description of our spiritual armor with these words: "And pray in the Spirit on all occasions with all kinds of prayers and requests. With this in mind, be alert and always keep on praying for all the saints" (verse 18). In addition to wearing the armor of God, we can look to the Holy Spirit for guidance, encouragement, and continual comfort.

Words
of
Encouragement

31

Praise Honors God

*Whoever offers praise glorifies Me, and to him who
orders his conduct aright I will show the salvation
of God (Psalm 50:23 NKJV).*

Have you tried and tried to get yourself out
of a dilemma, and nothing worked? If I
suggest you try praise, you might say,
"That would be hypocritical." I understand why you
might feel that way. At one time I would have given the
same reply. But I've learned that we are obeying Scripture
when we praise God regardless of our circumstances.
Praise brings comfort to our hearts, because praise takes
our eyes off our problem and focuses them on God.

Oswald Chambers says, "If we only praise when we
feel like praising, it is simply an undisciplined expression, but if we deliberately go over the neck of our dis-
inclination and offer the sacrifice of praise, we are
emancipated by our very statements."

It isn't that we manipulate God by praising Him
when things go wrong. God is *for* us. He doesn't withhold good things from His children.

It's our adversary who puts blocks in our way. He does everything he can to keep us from receiving the blessings God has promised us. He knows that praise will help to set us free. Praise doesn't always set us free from painful circumstances, but it can set us free from doubt and worry.

The psalmists repeatedly use such expressions as "Praise the Lord with me." Jack Hayford says, "Praise is your pathway through the mired circumstances of the present world. Your step will be uncertain and slide unless you recognize that your praises form stepping-stones by which the Father paves your way into the future purpose He has for you."

Praise honors God. It declares our trust in Him. It tells Him we delight in Him. Many years ago I thought God was so exalted that He didn't need our praise. But I've learned that God *delights* in our praises. And we need to hear ourselves praising Him.

In his book *Reflections on the Psalms*, C.S. Lewis says, "I think we delight to praise what we enjoy because praise not merely expresses, but completes the enjoyment." When you come upon a breathtakingly beautiful scene, you enjoy it more when you share it with a friend. You can't keep silent about it. Your description of the beauty of the scene finds expression in words of praise. Likewise, praise completes our enjoyment of God.

The Lord never *forces* us to do anything. He wants to *motivate* us to praise. When we see God as He really is, we *desire* to praise Him. That's probably why it was so natural and easy for the psalmists to praise God. They spent much time alone with Him and became intimately acquainted with Him. When they beheld His goodness and greatness, they could not hold back their expressions of praises.

In his book *Let Us Praise*, Judson Cornwall says, "Until we get a glimpse of who He is, we'll never be good praisers. We must see Him as gracious; we must see Him as merciful; we must see Him as plenteous in love and full of compassion."

If our church heritage or legalism has shown us a God who is like a stern policeman looking for some deed to punish, instead of a God of tender mercy and love, we will find it hard to praise Him. Or if we have such a lofty concept of God that we consider Him unapproachable, we will have difficulty praising Him.

As a young Christian, I fell into both of those categories. Then the Holy Spirit gave me a glimpse of God as He is. I'm still learning. I often pray, "Lord, help me to see You as You really are." My concept of God is clear enough now that I am able to praise Him freely as I worship Him during my daily quiet time. The more of His goodness I see, the more I want to praise Him.

When I take my eyes off God and focus on unpleasant circumstances, it becomes difficult to praise God with feeling. When conditions look threatening, I often feel more like complaining than praising. But praise, not complaints, can set me free and bring me comfort.

If praise comes with great effort, we know it's time to be still and let God remind us that He is our all-loving, all-powerful Father who wants only the best for us. It's time to remind ourselves of all He *has* done, what He *is* doing, and what He *will* do.

It's time for us to take a close look at Scriptures which tell of His goodness and greatness, time to meditate on certain Psalms or promises. When we see what David saw, we will be more likely to feel what David felt and do what David did: praise the Lord for who He is. Four times in Psalm 107 David says, "Let them give thanks to the LORD for his unfailing love." Meditating on God's goodness and love builds our faith.

Judson Cornwall says, "Praise is a God-given, scripturally taught channel of release for the emotions. It enables us to release pent-up feelings in a safe, positive fashion that blesses God and builds us up."

I hope we understand, however, that praise is more than expressing an emotional high. Praise declares our recognition of God's goodness. Praise serves to bring us into God's presence. Scripture tells us that the Lord inhabits the praises of His people: "But You are holy, who inhabit the praises of Israel" (Psalm 22:3 NKJV).

One of the strongest preventives is fear—fear of ourselves, fear of releasing our inner feelings, fear of what others may think. When we fully realize that Satan is the author of fear and that he uses this weapon to keep us from entering into the blessings of God through praise, perhaps we will let go of our reluctance to praise.

Let's declare with David, "I will exalt you, my God the King; I will praise your name for ever and ever. Every day I will praise you and extol your name for ever and ever" (Psalm 145:1,2). We may find ourselves comforted in situations which we thought were impossible to find comfort.

32

Saints in His Sight

*If anyone is in Christ, he is a new creation; the
old has gone, the new has come!*
(2 Corinthians 5:17).

Several years ago when I was visiting in another state, I met a lovely young woman who had heard a lot of legalistic teaching. She was a dedicated Christian, but she described herself as a sinner. She had never grasped the idea that the Father sees her as washed clean. Her desire was to live for the Lord, but the erroneous teaching she had heard and the memory of her past clung to her, making her feel guilty.

If someone asks you who you are, you may reply, "Oh, I'm just a sinner saved by grace."

Thirty years ago I might have given the same answer. But then one day I heard a minister call his congregation "saints." I thought, "What boldness! Everyone here probably is a Christian, but *saints?*"

I discovered from Scripture where he got his idea of calling us saints. The Christians of Bible times were called saints, and they were every bit as prone to stumbling as you and I. Since God shows no partiality, we too are saints in His sight.

Paul began many of his letters by addressing the Christians as saints. Even to the church at Corinth, Paul began his letter, ". . . to the church of God in Corinth, to those sanctified in Christ Jesus and called to be holy." If you've read the Corinthian letters, you know that those people did nothing to deserve the title of saints. They fell into all kinds of sin even after they accepted Christ.

Paul was about to write a letter specifically pointing out the nature of their sins. Why would he address the Corinthians as saints when he knew the depth of their sins? The answer is that Paul knew that the Corinthians had accepted the gift of salvation. They had been saved and sanctified—set apart for God's use—just as you and I have been. Paul knew that neither salvation nor sainthood depends on works, but upon accepting God's free gift.

When we repent of our sins and accept the gift of salvation, we are joined to Christ. From that time on, God no longer sees us as sinners but as His redeemed children. We become identified with Him. Our identification makes us totally acceptable to Christ. We are *righteous* in His sight. He calls us the salt of the earth and the light of the world (Matthew 5:13,14).

Paul reminded the Corinthians that they were once among the worst of sinners. Then he said, "But you were washed, you were sanctified, you were justified in the name of the Lord Jesus Christ" (1 Corinthians 6:11).

Over and over Paul reminded the Corinthians of who they were in Christ. That awareness—remembering who we are and whose we are—should be sufficient to turn us back to Christ and cause us to want to live wholly for Him.

In his book *Birthright*, Bible professor David Needham says, "The answer to the problem of sin is deeply rooted in the discovery of who a Christian actually is." When a Christian thinks of himself as a sinner, he is much more likely to fall into sin than if he realizes he is the temple of the living God. We act according to the way we see ourselves.

I'm not suggesting that we no longer sin. We will never reach sinless perfection until we are eternally with the Lord. But let's agree with who God says we are. Paul, inspired by the Holy Spirit, wrote, "For we know that our old self was crucified with him. . . . In the same way, count yourselves to be dead to sin but alive to God in Christ Jesus" (Romans 6:6,11). When we realize who we really are in Christ, we can have victory over sin. Christ lives within us so that "we are more than conquerors through him who loved us" (Romans 8:37).

We can say with Paul, "I have been crucified with Christ and I no longer live, but Christ lives in me. The life I live in the body, I live by faith in the Son of God" (Galatians 2:20). Because of our union with Christ, we died to sin and are alive to God (see chapters 6, 7, and 8 of Romans).

Since Christ is our life, the Father declares us righteous. "It is because of him that you are in Christ Jesus, who has become for us wisdom from God—that is, our righteousness, holiness and redemption" (1 Corinthians 1:30).

We are no longer the persons we were before we became Christians. David Needham says, "A Christian is not simply a person who gets forgiveness. . . . A Christian, in terms of his deepest identity, is a SAINT, a born again child of God, a divine masterpiece, a child of light, a citizen of heaven."

Paul writes, "For he has rescued us from the dominion of darkness and brought us into the kingdom of the Son he loves" (Colossians 1:13). He wants to conform us to His image so that He can express Himself through us. He has chosen us to be His representatives here on earth. That's who we really are—His saints, His representatives.

33

Resting in the Lord

Be empowered through your union with Him [Jesus];
draw your strength from Him . . .
(Ephesians 6:10 AMP).

It is our "union with Him," as Paul reminds us in the above verse, and not our fighting self-effort, that gives us the strength to be overcomers in a world of spiritual darkness.

When I was a girl, I lived on a farm. Daddy had a few grapevines. I never saw the branches straining to bear grapes. They just "rested" in the vine, and the grapes automatically came forth. It is when we're resting in the Lord, realizing we're His, that we are at peace. It is then that He can use us most effectively. If we strive, we only get in His way. He wants to accomplish His will in us and through us not by our straining and struggling and using our own efforts apart from Him, but by our abiding in Him.

Many of us are appalled by much that is going on in the world. Our biggest challenge may be to keep from getting so involved in trying to solve the problems that

143

we neglect our daily quiet times with the Lord. If we forget that God is still on His throne, we can drown in despair. What are we to do to keep the balance in our lives?

Personally, I sometimes find that a problem. When I've been around individuals who seem bent on informing us of the sordid details of the evil going on in the world, I come home feeling as if I need a spiritual bath.

After one such time I came home feeling especially downcast. I knew I had to do something about my feelings. I opened my Bible and read and meditated on the Scriptures assuring me of God's love for His own and His ultimate victory over sin. After a while I entered a place of rest in Him.

Of course, there is a place for concern for what is going on and for what the future holds. I especially appreciate what many influential leaders are doing to combat the evil in our world. We can support and pray for such leaders and organizations. We can pray for God to have mercy on our fallen world and for spiritual eyes to be opened. We can pray daily for ungodly political leaders to have their eyes opened to truth and be transformed, or to be put out of office and replaced by God-fearing leaders.

In the midst of it all, we need to remember that it is *individuals* who make up our world. It is *individuals* who are confused and hurting. In our concern for the world, let us not fail to focus on the fact that Christ died for *individuals*. He came to make us whole in every area of life. Through Him we have victory. In Him we have rest.

Somewhere I read about a concerned man who asked the Lord, "What is my responsibility?" The reply came, "Your part is simply to be in union with me, just as a branch abides in the vine." Jesus said, "I am the vine, you are the branches. He who abides in Me, and I in him, bears much fruit; for without Me you can do nothing" (John 15:5 NKJV).

In his book *The Adventure of Living*, Paul Tournier tells about a friend who rose from prayer one day and said, "I understand now. What I have to do is to put my signature at the foot of a blank page on which I will accept whatever God wishes to write. I cannot predict what He will put on this blank contract as my life proceeds—but I give my signature today." That's a good example of resting in the Lord, of being in union with Him.

When we trust the Lord with our problems and with the world's problems, we rest in the assurance that in His time, He will turn things around. Meanwhile, our part is to pray for His will to be done in us and through us. Paul Tournier says the more we surrender ourselves to God, the more time we will spend finding out what He wants, studying the Scriptures and getting to know Him better. Even though we're resting in the Lord, we're not passive in spirit, but active.

Dr. Tournier expresses it well when he calls this kind of living an adventure of faith. He says it's "exciting, difficult, exacting, but full of fresh turns and sudden surprises." Tournier goes on to say that this adventure of faith and surrender is not only for a few pious times, but for every minute of every day of our lives.

"Saying 'Yes' to God is saying 'Yes' to life, to all its problems and difficulties," says Tournier. When we remember that God is in charge, we know that nothing happens without His knowledge. Nothing takes Him by surprise.

Rufus Moseley said in his book *Manifest Victory* that he had learned the secret of living in union with God and abiding in His love. Then he "could even be in heavenly places while plowing with a mule . . . in death cells, in all places of need." Moseley said he had received "the master key of the Kingdom of Heaven, abiding in union with Jesus." He went on to say when we receive that key, "heaven can and will be everywhere as we go in His love, manifesting His love and nothing but His love."

I don't claim to be that far along in my walk with the Lord. It's a goal to aim for as we discipline ourselves to spend more time in conscious union with Him. That would be living a life of rest in the Lord while doing spiritual battle in the world.

More than 50 years ago, C. B. McAfee wrote this inspiring hymn which reminds us to rest in the Lord:

There is a place of quiet rest,
Near to the heart of God,
A place where sin cannot molest,
Near to the heart of God.
Jesus, blest Redeemer,
Sent from the heart of God,
Hold us who wait before Thee,
Near to the heart of God.

Words
of
Confidence

34

God Is for Us

I know and rest in confidence upon it that the Lord
will maintain the cause of the afflicted, and will serve
justice for the poor and needy . . .
(Psalm 140:12 AMP).

ife consists of change. Obstacles often attend
those changes. We find that some circumstances are beyond our control. God may use
circumstances and trials to put us in a better position to
receive His blessings. Even when we face disappointments,
we can be confident of God's love and kindness.

We can always be confident that God is for us,
never against us. He has a plan for our lives. Regardless
of what may come, we can trust God to fit everything
into His perfect plan for us. He will be faithful to direct
our paths. Solomon reminds us: "Trust in the LORD
with all your heart, and lean not on your own understanding; in all your ways acknowledge Him, and He
shall direct your paths" (Proverbs 3:5 NKJV).

We face times when we don't know what to do. In
those times we need only ask God for guidance. James

tells us, "If any of you lacks wisdom, he should ask God, who gives generously to all without finding fault, and it will be given to him" (James 1:5).

God's plans and purposes never fail. He fits all our circumstances into His plan to bring us to greater spiritual maturity, and, in the end, to greater joy.

Sometimes we may feel like giving up on ourselves, but God never will. We can declare with Paul, "Being confident of this, that he who began a good work in you will carry it on to completion until the day of Christ Jesus" (Philippians 1:6).

God wants us to begin every day with hope and joy, knowing that He has opportunities in store for us. He will reveal those opportunities as we move through each day, each month, each year, reading His Word, praying, seeking His guidance, and following His leading. Life is God's greatest gift to us. His desire is that we look to Him in complete confidence in His power, wisdom, and goodness for the unwrapping of that gift.

"No good thing does he withhold from those whose walk is blameless," says the psalmist in Psalm 84:11. He wants us to ask Him for those things, believing that it is His desire to supply them. His design is that we have a part with Him in His plan of giving.

One way we fulfill God's plan is to live in joy. Charles Spurgeon says that Christians should be happy people. "It is good for our God, it gives Him great honor among men when we are glad. It is good for us, it makes us strong. 'The joy of the LORD is your strength' (Nehemiah 8:10 KJV). It is good for the ungodly when they see Christians glad, they long to be believers themselves. It is good for our fellow Christians; it comforts them and tends to cheer them. . . .

"It is an unfortunate thing for the Christian to become melancholy. If there is any man in the world that has a right to have a bright, clear face and to have a flashing eye, it is the man whose sins are forgiven him."

Let us not get so caught up in the cares of life that we forget the most important thing—that we belong to Christ and that because of Him we can be filled with hope, joy, and confidence.

The seventeenth-century poet and writer John Milton had joy in spite of hardships. Circumstances sometimes shook his faith. Blindness struck him at the age of 44. His first wife died that same year. He remarried four years later, and his second wife died 15 months later.

In spite of all his heartaches, Milton wrote and inspired others. His gladness is reflected in his hymn "Let Us with Gladsome Mind":

Let us with a gladsome mind
Praise the Lord, for He is kind:
For His mercies shall endure,
Ever faithful, ever sure.

Let us sound His name abroad,
For of gods He is the God:
For His mercies shall endure,
Ever faithful, ever sure.
He, with all-commanding might,
Filled the new-made world with light:

For His mercies shall endure,
Ever faithful, ever sure.

All things living He doth feed;
His full hand supplies their need:
For His mercies shall endure,
Ever faithful, ever sure.

Let us then with gladsome mind
Praise the Lord, for He is kind:
For His mercies shall endure,
Ever faithful, ever sure.

God's plan was fulfilled in John Milton's life as he yielded himself to the lordship of Christ, letting His glory shine through. Just as surely as God's plan was fulfilled in Milton and other well-known men and women, His plan can be fulfilled in you and me.

Let's expect God's blessings upon us as we move through each day of life. He has prepared in advance for us to do certain things, fulfilling His plan and purpose for us. He will make a way for us when there seems to be no way.

35

Living Above the Gray

Do not throw away your confidence; it will be richly rewarded (Hebrews 10:35).

Some of us have taken off in an airplane when the sky was so overcast that we could see nothing but gray clouds in every direction. But soon we were flying above the clouds into brilliant sunlight. How often we've wished we could rise that easily above life's situations!

Most of us meet often with gray days. Sometimes we feel that we *live* with gray days. The only way we can live through them is to experience a continuous flow of God's grace. It might help to remind ourselves of the Lord's words to the apostle Paul, and know that they apply to us: "My grace is sufficient for you." We can put our confidence in those words. The grace of God is always sufficient.

We would like for all of life to be stress-free, but it seldom is. It's in the midst of life's struggles that we learn to depend on God. Most of us are slow to discover that our problems usually come from within, not from without.

In times of stress we're particularly aware of our need for quietness with the Lord. Unfortunately, those are the very times we find it most difficult to achieve inner quiet. Even though I practice a daily quiet time with the Lord, I find that when a stressful situation arises, it's hard to still my inner self and feel His presence. The cares of the world often cause my thoughts to stray.

That's when we have to accept by faith that the Lord is with us, and that He is able to meet our needs. Lory Basham Jones says in her book *Hearing God*, "Serenity is a continual effort until it becomes a habit." It begins with bringing our thoughts into captivity to the obedience of Christ (2 Corinthians 10:5). Lory Jones envisions the Lord saying, "Wherever your body happens to be, you can be in as close communion with Me as if you were in a dynamic prayer meeting."

In her book *Experiencing the Depths of Jesus Christ*, seventeenth-century Jean Guyon says we must believe that every circumstance of life comes to us with the permission of the Father and is exactly what we need. If we recognize the hand of our loving Father in every experience, we'll understand that He will bring something good from it, regardless of what happens.

How easily we forget that God is in control and that He is *for* us. And "if God is for us, who can be against us?" (Romans 8:31).

Three times in the first chapter of Joshua, the Lord told Joshua, "Be strong and courageous." In verse 9 He added, "Do not be terrified; do not be discouraged, for the LORD your God will be with you wherever you go."

Of course, you and I are not leading a multitude of people into a new land, as Joshua was. But we have other responsibilities that may sometimes seem almost that great to us. The same words of encouragement spoken to Joshua apply to us. God wants us never to feel alone, but to have confidence in His ability to provide for our every need.

The Lord would say to us, "Do not allow your spiritual enemy to cause you to doubt the presence of the Almighty One. I will not be late with the solution. Trust Me. Bring your cares to me. I am greater than any problem you have. Rest in Me. Trust in Me with all your heart and lean not on your own understanding" (see Proverbs 3:5).

In his book *Where Is God When It Hurts?* Phillip Yancey says, "He has promised supernatural strength to nourish our spirits, even if our physical suffering goes unrelieved. He has joined us." Regardless of the nature of our trials, God's promise is the same: He is present to strengthen and encourage us. We cannot escape the promises of God. They are as true for us as they were for the people to whom they first were written.

36
God Hears Us

This is the confidence we have in approaching God: that
if we ask anything according to his will, he hears us.
And if we know that he hears us—whatever we ask—we
know that we have what we asked of him
(1 John 5:14,15).

It isn't easy to be confident that God hears us in the midst of humdrum routine and hectic activities. How can we be aware of God's nearness while checking things off our endless to-do lists? The apostle Paul said we are to pray constantly. But how can we?

A busy young mother confessed that her prayers are usually, "God, help me!" Many of us probably feel that way at times. Someone said, "God is happy to communicate with us 'on the run,' but having an extended quiet time with Him can deepen our relationship." I'm sure you and I agree.

God never wants us to think of prayer as something we "have to do," but as an opportunity to talk with Him as our loving Father. As good parents are delighted when their little children come to them to discuss their problems and desires, so our heavenly Father is delighted when we come to Him with whatever we have on our hearts. Jesus encouraged His followers to pray as little children, simply and trustingly.

A certain minister said, "I've found if I don't take time to just be in the presence of the Lord in the morning, the rest of my day is shot. We don't have to say anything to Him; just sit and listen to Him."

The psalmist David is a good example of someone who listened to God and spoke his heart to Him. On one occasion David prayed, "Let me understand the teaching of your precepts; then I will meditate on your wonders" (Psalm 119:27).

One good way to talk to God is to pray the Scriptures, making them personal for our own lives. For instance, you may be reading Psalm 1: "Blessed is the man who does not walk in the counsel of the wicked or stand in the way of sinners or sit in the seat of mockers" (verse 1). Your prayer might be, "Lord, I choose not to follow the counsel of those who dishonor You. Help me never to live in any way as those who do not love You. May I never be a mocker or treat anyone with scorn or contempt. Thank You that You promise to bless those who do not walk, stand, or sit where the ungodly live."

Or let's say you're reading Psalm 145: "I will exalt you, my God the King; I will praise your name for ever and ever. Every day I will praise you and extol your name for ever and ever (verses 1 and 2). You can make those words your prayer: "Lord, I recognize You as my

God and King. Help me to praise Your name every day in all my ways."

Maybe you're feeling restless and doubtful. You might pray Psalm 62:5,6, and meditate on the words: "Find rest, O my soul, in God alone; my hope comes from him. He alone is my rock and my salvation; he is my fortress, I will not be shaken." And Psalm 63:3,4: "Because your love is better than life, my lips will glorify you. I will praise you as long as I live, and in your name I will lift up my hands."

A small congregation gathered one Sunday morning, weary of battling harsh weather. Everyone seemed to be discouraged. The pastor suggested that they begin the service by thanking God for something. As everyone began to name something for which they were thankful, rejoicing filled the sanctuary. Giving thanks often brings feelings of thankfulness.

Remembering the past goodness of God gives us cause to praise God in the seeming absence of present things to praise Him for. Perhaps David was remembering his past blessings when he said, "I will sing to the LORD all my life; I will sing praise to my God as long as I live. May my meditation be pleasing to him, as I rejoice in the LORD" (Psalm 104:33,34).

When you are in need of feeling more of God's love, you may want to pray Ephesians 3:16-19, personalizing it like this: "I pray that out of His glorious riches He may strengthen me with power through His Spirit in my inner being, so that Christ may dwell in my heart through faith—that I, being rooted and established in love, may have power, together with all the saints, to grasp how wide and long and high and deep is the love of Christ, and to know this love that surpasses knowledge—that I may be filled to the measure of all the fullness of God."

Whatever your need, God has an answer in His Word.

37

Everything for Good

We have one who speaks to the Father in our defense—Jesus Christ, the Righteous One. He is the atoning sacrifice for our sins . . . (1 John 2:1,2).

In the beginning of Billy Graham's ministry, he said he was so filled with doubts that when he stood to preach and made a statement, he would ask himself, "I wonder if that is really true. Can I say that sincerely?"

One day he took his Bible up into the mountains, opened it and got on his knees, and prayed, "Father, I cannot understand many things in this Book. I cannot come intellectually all the way, but I accept it by faith to be the authoritative, inspired Word of the living God."

Circumstances in our lives may cause us to question whether we really believe the promises in the Bible. We want to. They sound good—almost too good to be true. Yet we know that God's Word is eternal, that He is a loving, forgiving, unchanging God.

All of us have read or quoted Romans 8:28: "We know that in all things God works for the good of those who love him, who have been called according to his purpose." We know this truth intellectually, but sometimes we have difficulty accepting its truth when it seems as if things are going against us.

Commenting on Romans 8:28, James Kennedy writes, "God makes it clear that whatever event comes upon us, no matter how grim or ghastly in itself, as soon as it touches our lives, the hand of God will reach down and take it captive. And God will not let it go until it yields up its treasure to our soul. That is the promise of the Almighty."

Dr. Kennedy goes on to emphasize that things do not work out for our good *by themselves*, but it is God who causes them to work together for our good.

Observing the same verse of Scripture, Oswald Chambers said, "The circumstances of a saint's life are ordained of God. In the life of a saint there is no such thing as chance. . . . All your circumstances are in the hand of God; therefore never think it strange concerning the circumstances you are in."

We may be prone to stop when we read "saints," and say, "That leaves me out. I'm not worthy to be called a saint." But throughout the New Testament Christians are referred to as saints. If we belong to Christ, He calls us saints, and all His promises are ours. We can take Him at His Word.

We may be tempted to wonder why God allows certain things to happen to us if we're saints. Charles Stanley writes, "You may wonder why a certain tragedy had to happen, but you need never doubt the goodness of God's sovereign will. He sees the beginning and end of your life, and only He can transform your tragedies into something of lasting value."

Author Elisabeth Elliot, who suffered many heartaches, said that nothing is a waste with God. He takes everything, even the slightest detail, and works it all together for our good. No matter what we are facing, the Lord has a plan in mind for our future. We can talk to Him about our doubts and fears, and He will strengthen and encourage us.

All of us need to be continually reminded of God's personal love for us. I was blessed by this reminder when I read the following paragraph in Neil Anderson's book *Victory over the Darkness*:

> The primary truth you need to know about God in order for your faith to remain strong is that His love and acceptance is unconditional. When your walk of faith is strong, God loves you. When your walk of faith is weak, God loves you. When you're strong one moment and weak the next, strong one day and weak the next, God loves you. God's love for you is the great eternal constant in the midst of all the inconsistencies of your daily walk.

You may have read about the great palace near Madrid, Spain. Kings and queens of Spain are buried there. When the building was under construction, the architect designed an arch much larger than any built before. The entire weight of the church's roof would rest on that arch.

The king insisted that the weight of the roof would be more than the arch could bear. So he ordered the architect to build a column from the floor to the center of the arch to prop it up.

After the king died, the architect revealed that he had left a quarter-inch space between the top of the column and the arch it was supposedly supporting. Hundreds of years later, visitors who come to the palace find that the arch still has not sagged even a quarter of an inch. The architect's plan for the palace proved to be perfect.

So it is with God's plan for our lives: It is perfect. We can affirm with Paul, "He who began a good work in you will carry it on to completion until the day of Christ Jesus" (Philippians 1:6). We can always take God at His Word.

Words
of
Faith

38

Ruled by Faith

Faith comes by hearing, and hearing by the word
of God (Romans 10:17 NKJV).

One of Satan's favorite weapons against us as
believers is doubt. He knows that if he can
get us to doubt we may give up on God and
quit trying to live the Christian life. Not only does our
spiritual adversary want to discourage us from trusting
God, but he also delights in making us miserable, simply
because we belong to Christ.

There are two sources to turn to when doubt begins
to overtake us—prayer, and reading and meditating on
God's written Word. We want faith, not doubt, to be
the rule of our lives.

When our level of trust runs low, we need not think
that God has abandoned us. Our all-wise and loving
heavenly Father understands. He is present to help us
overcome our doubts. We can tell Him all about how
we feel, and He will listen not with a critical ear but
with kindness.

We accomplish nothing by denying our doubts.

God knows them anyway. "Honesty breaks the patterns of doubt," says Charles Stanley. As we spend more time reading God's Word and communing with Him in prayer, we will learn more about Him. And we will eventually discover that we have no need to let doubt linger in our minds and control us.

Doubt is a temptation to doubt God's Word. We never reach the point of rising above temptation. Jesus Himself suffered temptation but remained faithful. Most of us are not tempted to commit gross sins, but we often are tempted to question or distrust God. Doubt is our opportunity to prove God's faithfulness to us.

Peter expresses it like this: "These [trials and temptations] have come so that your faith—of greater worth than gold, which perishes even though refined by fire—may be proved genuine and may result in praise, glory and honor when Jesus Christ is revealed" (1 Peter 1:7).

"Temptation is a part of the process that brings about our development and conformity to the Lord Jesus Christ," says Paul Sexton in *The Banner*. "In His omniscience, God knows what is necessary to accomplish our perfection. The fire and circumstances that seemingly take us unawares may appear to be unjustifiable as far as we are concerned, but nonetheless God permits them."

God never brings about temptations. It is not His nature to initiate them, but He does allow them. However, He will never allow us to be tempted beyond our ability to endure. Paul makes this clear: "No temptation has seized you except what is common to man. And God is faithful; he will not let you be tempted beyond what you can bear. But when you are tempted, he will also provide a way out so that you can stand up under it" (1 Corinthians 10:13).

When we are tempted to doubt, we can be sure there is a way out. God only asks that we stand firm and look to Him instead of to what seems inevitable.

Remember how Abraham was tempted to doubt when God promised him a son in his advanced years? In spite of Abraham's doubts, God fulfilled His promise. Isaac was born to Abraham when he was 100 years old.

Can you imagine the doubt that filled the minds of Mary and Martha when Jesus told them their brother Lazarus would rise from the dead when he had been dead four days? Oswald Chambers says personal belief cannot emerge in us until "a personal need arises out of a personal problem." It is in times of our greatest need that God can strengthen us most. When our days seem darkest and the most hopeless, God is still present to answer.

The writer to the Hebrews assures us: "God has said, 'Never will I leave you; never will I forsake you.' So we say with confidence, 'The Lord is my helper; I will not be afraid'" (Hebrews 13:5).

How often we trust each other,
And only doubt our Lord.
We take the word of mortals,
And yet distrust His word;
But, oh, what light and glory
Would shine o'er all our days,
If we always would remember
God means just what He says!

—Anonymous

39

An Attitude of Hope

*You have been given fullness in Christ, who is the
head over every power and authority
(Colossians 2:10).*

The southern tip of Africa used to be called
"Cape of Tempests." Its adverse weather
conditions caused sailors great anxiety and
many deaths. But a certain Portuguese man with a
hopeful attitude determined to find a safer route
through those rough seas. He did, and the area was
renamed the "Cape of Good Hope."

You and I are bound to experience adverse circumstances and situations. We often are unable to change
them, but we can change our outlook toward them
through a change of attitude. Anxiety may be turned to
hope when we decide to develop a hopeful attitude and
a renewed belief in God.

Developing a hopeful attitude may be a challenge
when things around us are less than desirable. A man
known for his positive thinking confessed that he was
not always positive. One night after making a speech he

170

returned to his motel room and went to the ice machine for some ice water. There he met a stranger who asked, "How are you?"

"Pretty good," he replied.

"Pretty good? Is that all you can say?" the stranger asked. "You look like a healthy fellow." Then he held up a book and said, "You ought to read this book."

The "positive thinker" felt too humiliated to tell the joyful stranger he was the author of that book.

Some people seem to have been born with a hopeful mental attitude. I wasn't. I have to work at it, especially when I'm not feeling up to par. I've found that singing helps. One evening when I'd felt downcast much of the day, I came across the words of the song "What a Friend." I sang a portion of it a few times and soon felt much better.

WHAT A FRIEND

What a Friend we have in Jesus,
All our sins and griefs to bear!
What a privilege to carry
Everything to God in prayer. . . .
Can we find a friend so faithful
Who will all our sorrows share?
Jesus knows our every weakness;
Take it to the Lord in prayer.

Shower time is a good time to sing hymns or choruses. While soap and water washes our bodies clean, joyful singing can wash our minds clean and prepare us for a positive day. Listening to praise tapes at every opportunity is also helpful. I try to remember to keep one going when I'm cooking or washing dishes. It keeps me from dwelling on useless thoughts.

Disappointment can set us up for pessimistic think-ing unless we remind ourselves that God is in charge. "If your hopes are being disappointed just now it means they are being purified," says Oswald Chambers. "There is nothing noble the human mind has ever hoped for or dreamed of that will not be fulfilled."

Hopes and dreams are often the key to a hopeful attitude. "Dreaming will not only change the dreamer, but it can also extend one's real horizons beyond any-thing that could have been imagined," say Tom Fatjo and Keith Miller in their book *With No Fear of Failure.*

Of course the best book we can read to help us develop a hopeful outlook is the Bible. For example: "This is the day the LORD has made; let us rejoice and be glad in it" (Psalm 118:24). If we rejoice in the Lord and in each day He makes, how can we be anything but positive in our attitude?

Too often we allow the things at hand, or the regrettable things of our past, or things we fear may happen, to occupy much of our thinking. Realizing this tendency of our nature, someone said, "It's no wonder we need the time to retreat and readjust our mental attitudes." Our best retreat may be simply to withdraw from whatever we're doing and take time to be aware of the Lord's presence.

The Bible tells us to "be transformed by the renew-ing of your mind" (Romans 12:2). We are transformed as we both read and meditate on the words of Scripture. Keeping God's Word and His promises foremost in our minds while going about each day's work is not always easy, but the Holy Spirit is present to help us. The Lord says He came to give us abundant life, and abundant life includes living with a hopeful attitude. Our greatest hope is in knowing that Christ lives within us: He "is the hope of glory. . . . For in Christ all the fullness of the Deity lives in bodily form, and you have been given fullness in Christ, who is the head over every power and authority" (Colossians 1:27; 2:9,10).

As the Portuguese man found a safe route around the southern tip of Africa, can you and I find a safe route around the pessimism that surrounds us and instead live our lives with a hopeful attitude? With God's help we can.

40

Our Loving, Faithful God

The LORD your God is with you, he is mighty to save. He will take great delight in you, he will quiet you with his love, he will rejoice over you with singing (Zephaniah 3:17).

A popular Christian writer and speaker tells of the poor relationship she had with her father in her childhood. She seldom had the privilege of sitting on his lap or communicating with him in any way. Feeling shut away from him, she was a lonely little girl, always longing for a father's love but never receiving it.

When she reached adulthood, she identified her heavenly Father with her earthly father. For a long time God seemed faraway, awesome, and powerful, but a God who didn't care about her.

At last she discovered that her heavenly Father's likeness could be seen in the life of Jesus—always full of love and care. Her new concept of God didn't come overnight. It took much time for the light to dawn in her heart that God is always accessible and interested in every detail of our lives.

All of us need to know that we are cared for by a loving, faithful God. But for one reason or another, many of us have not felt that way.

In his book *God Is My Delight*, Phillip Keller says the love of God has been the subject of more sermons than any other subject. But he says that far too often it is nothing more than a doctrine. "It is one thing to talk about the love of Christ in a rather detached way.... It is quite another to encounter that love expressed in the person of Christ."

Sometimes we have difficulty grasping things from God's perspective. Our past experiences or teachings, or the world in which we live, hinder our understanding of the truth of God's personal love for us. As a result, some of us sometimes battle feelings of unworthiness.

We have to realize that we are worthy through Christ and Him alone. He sees us differently from the way we see ourselves. It is with great difficulty that most of us grasp the truth that God delights in us and rejoices over us.

The word *delight* reportedly occurs in some form about 80 times in the Bible. In many of those instances it refers to God's delight in His people. This means that each of us is special in God's sight.

Even before He created the world, God planned for you and me. He chose us and adopted us into His family. Jesus paid the ultimate price for us when He came to earth as a man and died on the cross to redeem us. We have real worth in the eyes of our heavenly Father.

God's love "flows from Him to us in a steady stream of endless self-giving, self-sacrifice, selflessness that has no parallel upon the planet," says author Phillip Keller. We are set apart to God for His loving purposes.

God is not only our loving Father, but He wants to be our best friend and companion in all of life's challenges. He delights in our fellowship. He wants us to share with Him every joy and every sorrow. No one understands us as He does. He understands all about us, and He still loves us with an unconditional love. He knows why we act and think as we do. He never condemns us, but only encourages us.

If we have difficulty realizing that God delights in us, we might do well to ask Him to help us see ourselves from His perspective. We can look in the Scriptures for passages that help us to realize the great extent of God's love for us. Meditating on such verses can do much for us. Even when we feel unworthy, we are worthy in God's sight because of Christ.

The Lord wants us to get a clear picture of His care. Over and over in the Scriptures He emphasizes the assurance of His presence.

One of my favorite Scriptures is Psalm 91. Sometimes when I'm awakened in the night, and sleep eludes me, I quote the parts of that Psalm that come to my mind. Sometimes I'm half-asleep by the time I finish quoting the first two verses:

"He who dwells in the shelter of the Most High will rest in the shadow of the Almighty. I will say of the LORD, He is my refuge and my fortress, my God, in whom I trust" (Psalm 91:1,2). Only of a God who cares for us and delights in us could we affirm such trust.

Words
of
Thanksgiving

41

A Thankful Heart

It is good to give thanks to the LORD, and to sing
praises to Your name, O Most High
(Psalm 92:1 NKJV).

Observing a day of thanksgiving dates back to the early days of Israel when the people assembled every year for the feast of thanksgiving. They called it the Feast of Harvest (see Exodus 23:16). Why did they observe such a day? Their celebrations were for the same reasons ours are to be—to acknowledge God's goodness and to give Him thanks for His blessings. We need not look at conditions, but at God and His faithfulness for reasons to celebrate a time of thanksgiving.

By celebrating such thanksgiving, we acknowledge our own helplessness and our dependence upon God as our Creator and Sustainer of life. God has not failed us. In spite of all the evil and injustice going on in our country, we still have many reasons to thank God. The main reason is that "because of the Lord's great love we are not consumed, for his compassions never fail" (Lamentations 3:22).

The enemy of our souls is working overtime to tempt people to doubt that God is still in control and that His promises apply to us today. If we allow him to, the enemy will fill us with despair and a spirit of thanklessness. Let's remind ourselves as often as necessary that the devil is a liar and a defeated foe.

Regardless of whether we deserve God's blessings, His faithfulness continues. "If we are faithless, he will remain faithful, for he cannot disown himself" (2 Timothy 2:13).

We may be powerless to change the circumstances around us, but we can rejoice in God, with whom all things are possible. Jack Hayford reminds us that "no situation is hopeless as long as we allow the power of the Spirit to fill our weaknesses." We can "have a fresh sense of God's peace in the face of present circumstances, and a renewed hope for a better tomorrow from Him who holds our future in His hands."

For us who know God, every day is a thanksgiving day. We may experience trials and troubles, but we can be sure they are not from God. They come either from our own confusion or from our dark enemy. God does not cause our troubles, but He is with us in the midst of them. He uses our trials to purify us and to draw us closer to Himself.

Many situations arise to tempt us to worry. The best way to dispel worry and anxiety is to give thanks to God for His unfailing goodness. Remembering that God is still God can bring our thoughts back into proper focus.

I read about a little girl who was asked to give

thanks at the table. When she thanked God for a beautiful day, her mother reminded her that it was raining. The child's reply demonstrated unbelievable wisdom: "Mother, never judge a day by its weather."

Neither do you and I need to judge what we see as final reality. If we do, we may become hopeless concerning our future. In an article written by Billy Graham for *Decision Magazine* a few years ago, he said, "We need to dream big dreams, embrace great principles, renew our hope. But above all, we need to believe in the Christ who alone can give total meaning and an ultimate goal for our lives." We can dream big dreams, embrace great principles, and renew our hope only by keeping our eyes on the Lord and thanking Him for what He has done and is able to do now and in the future.

As I was reading about thanksgiving, I came across this definition of the art of thanksgiving written about 35 years ago by a man by the name of Wilfred Peterson. "The art of thanksgiving is thanks*living*. It is gratitude in action. . . . It is thanking God for the gift of life by living it triumphantly. . . . It is adding to your prayers of thanksgiving, acts of thanks*living*."

The psalmist says, "It is good to give thanks to the LORD, and to sing praises to Your name, O Most High; to declare Your lovingkindness in the morning, and Your faithfulness every night" (Psalm 92:1,2 NKJV).

Let us rejoice in the steadfast, unchanging love of God our Father. Let us look for reasons to thank and praise God. He is still on His throne. He will never leave us nor forsake us.

As His mercies are new every morning, so can His written Word hold fresh meaning for us every day, as we ask the Holy Spirit to reveal new insights to us. Then we will find new reasons to have a truly thankful heart.

42

An Attitude of Gratitude

Every good and perfect gift is from above, coming down from the Father of the heavenly lights, who does not change like shifting shadows (James 1:17).

Am I truly thankful? What am I thankful for? May none of us ever be like a man whom a famous preacher told about. The preacher had spoken on the subject "The Attitude of Gratitude." Afterward a man who had heard him speak approached him and said, "I have nothing to be glad about. Everything is going badly for me."

The preacher took out a large sheet of paper and wrote at the top of one side "Things That Make Me Happy" and on the other side "Things That Make Me Unhappy."

He handed the paper to the man and said, "Since you're so unhappy, let's start with the unhappy side." He quickly filled the page.

"Now," said the preacher, "turn the paper over and let's practice the attitude of gratitude. What do you have to be grateful for?"

"Not a thing," said the man.

"You have your eyes. Think what life would be like if you couldn't see." Then they named the other parts of the man's body: Ears, arms, legs, etc.

Finally the man grinned and said, "I get the point."

Some time later the preacher met the man again, he then said, "I've finished filling the happy side of that paper. Now I'm crossing out the things on the unhappy side."

The early Pilgrims were thankful simply for survival. You and I have much more than survival to be thankful for, but we often take our blessings for granted. If you are fortunate enough to sit at a table laden with food every day, are you thankful for the blessing of food, remembering that half the world goes to bed hungry every night?

When the children of Israel were wandering in the desert on their way to the Promised Land, God promised to supply their needs, and He did. One thing He did was to send manna every morning. They appreciated it for a long while, but then they started complaining that they were tired of it.

A time of thanksgiving gives us the opportunity to take a closer look at our attitudes and ask ourselves if we have grown so accustomed to our blessings that we have forgotten to be thankful. As someone said, "The Thanksgiving holiday does not change our circumstances, but the Thanksgiving state of mind can change our attitude toward our circumstances."

An event in the life of Matthew Henry, the great Bible commentator, illustrates how attitudes can improve our outlook on what happens to us. One day thieves robbed him. Afterward he wrote something like this in his diary: "I'm thankful that I've never been robbed before. I'm thankful that I was only robbed and not killed. I'm thankful that although they took everything I had, it wasn't much. I'm thankful that it was I who was robbed and not I who robbed."

What are we thankful for? When we get into our cars to go most anywhere we want to go, do we give thanks for transportation? Many people in the world cannot afford even a bicycle. I want to remind myself often that everything I have and all that I am is a gift from God.

I think first of the gift of salvation. I accepted the Lord as my personal Savior when I was 11 years old. I've never doubted or regretted that decision. But I'm certainly not as thankful as I could be. I'm especially aware of the greatness of that blessing when I realize that millions of people have never even heard the gospel.

I'm thankful to live in a land where the gospel is preached, and for having been brought up in a Christian home where the thought of not going to church on Sunday never crossed our minds.

I'm thankful for Christian friends and churches and the freedom of worship. It's hard for us to realize that many people in our world do not have the opportunity of worship as we do. Some have been ostracized from their families for choosing to follow Christ.

Let's join Abraham Lincoln in remembering, "The year that is drawing to its close has been filled with the blessing of fruitful fields and healthful skies—they are the gracious gifts of the Most High God!"

43

Always Thankful

Give thanks in all circumstances, for this is God's will for you in Christ Jesus (1 Thessalonians 5:18).

As an elementary schoolteacher, I had the periodic task of decorating my classroom bulletin board. One day near Thanksgiving one of my third-graders watched while I put the letters "Give Thanks" on our bulletin board. "Mrs. Shropshire, I think you made a mistake," he said. "It should say 'Thanksgiving.'"

I used the occasion to explain that we celebrate Thanksgiving because we want to give thanks to the Lord for His goodness to us. I wonder if we sometimes forget to be thankful to God for His goodness when we're in the midst of unpleasant circumstances.

"We have been the recipients of the choicest bounties of heaven," wrote Abraham Lincoln in his Thanksgiving Proclamation in 1863. Of course, Mr. Lincoln referred to our nation. But we can say the same about our individual lives. When we stop looking at our circumstances and enumerate our blessings, we may be surprised to see what the Lord has done for us.

The psalmist David said, "I will extol the LORD at all times; his praise will always be on my lips. . . . Glorify the LORD with me; let us exalt his name together" (Psalm 34:1,3). When David spoke these words, he had no human reason to praise God, but he knew who was in control of his life, and he thanked Him.

We are all familiar with the verse written by the apostle Paul, "Give thanks in all circumstances." With a puzzled look someone asked, "Did the Holy Spirit really inspire Paul to write that? Everything in my life is going wrong. Why should I give thanks?"

Giving thanks helps us to take our eyes off ourselves and focus them on God and His love and power. One day recently when I felt apprehensive about a certain situation, my eyes lit on Jeremiah 29:11 from The Living Bible: "I know the plans I have for you, says the Lord. They are plans for good and not for evil, to give you a future and a hope."

I relaxed, knowing that God would be with me in the situation. I knew without a doubt that I need not fear, but could give thanks to God for His care. I knew that God would work out His plan and that it would be "for good and not for evil." And He did just that.

"Giving thanks keeps us aware of God's presence," says Charles Stanley. "By thanking God in our rough situations, we heighten our sense of His redemptive involvement in our trials. We have help. We have His presence. . . . He is there to listen, comfort, and strengthen us."

If I could always remember that nothing can thwart God's purpose, I could *always* give thanks as Paul says. But in this world so many things distract our attention from Him and fill us with doubt. When we give thanks regardless of our circumstances, we demonstrate our faith in God.

It's easy to trust God and thank Him when everything is going the way we want it to. But if I never have to trust God when the way looks rough, I never have the opportunity to strengthen my faith. If I receive every request as soon as I ask for it, I have no need to develop my patience (which I confess is usually in short supply). So God is teaching me to trust that He knows the best timing for everything. When I rest in that assurance, I can give thanks from a sincere heart.

Poet A. L. Waring expresses the thought of God's timing in these words:

> *I love to think that God appoints*
> *My portion day by day;*
> *Events of life are in His hand,*
> *And I would only say,*
> *Appoint them in Thine own good time,*
> *And in Thine own best way.*

The origin of Thanksgiving in America goes back to Governor Bradford of the Plymouth Colony in 1621. You know the difficulties the Pilgrims endured those first winters in their new land. But in spite of all their hardships, they observed a November day to give thanks to God for His goodness and care.

We often talk about the Thanksgiving season, referring to the calendar year. But for Christians, thanksgiving is to be year-round because a spirit of thanksgiving pervades our whole life. We want to communicate constantly to God our gratitude for His loving care and provision.

Someone said, "The constant exercise of thanksgiving is a frontal attack on the fluctuations of experience and emotions." Our low feelings diminish when we focus on God and all He *has* done, *is* doing, and *will* do for us. The beginning of every day can be a reminder of how indebted we are to our heavenly Father. The very air that we breathe is a gift from Him.

The apostle Paul said, "He who did not spare his own Son, but gave him up for us all—how will he not also, along with him, graciously give us all things?" (Romans 8:32). If we believe that truth with all our hearts, surely we will always be filled with gratitude. Giving thanks will come easily and naturally.

44

God's Bountiful Supply

Enter his gates with thanksgiving and his courts with
praise; give thanks to him and praise his name
(Psalm 100:4).

I recently read that the Pilgrims' original
Thanksgiving celebration in America was
not their first such celebration. They had
been raised in a culture which observed a time of praise
each year at harvesttime. They thanked God for the
year's harvest and His bountiful supply.

Jack Hayford relates that the people of England celebrated a feast known as "harvest home" when the last
of their harvest was gathered in.

With that in mind, more than a century ago Henry
Alford wrote the hymn "Come, Ye Thankful People" to
lead his congregation in praise on their day of thanksgiving when the harvest had been gathered in.

> Come, ye thankful people, come,
> Raise the song of harvest-home:
> All is safely gathered in

Ere the winter storms begin.
God, our Maker, doth provide
For our wants to be supplied:
Come to God's own temple, come,
Raise the song of harvest-home.

You and I may not be able to relate precisely to their hymn of thanksgiving, since our lifestyles are so different. But we can show our thanks to God in ways which are natural for us. Surely we have much more to be thankful for than the early Pilgrims had—more conveniences, more opportunities, more of so many things.

God is no less our Sustainer of life than He was to the Pilgrims. But we often forget that it is by His hand that we are fed. We are dependent on God not only for every morsel of food we eat, but for every breath of air we take.

Paul reminds us to "give thanks in all circumstances, for this is God's will for you in Christ Jesus" (1 Thessalonians 5:18). We notice that Paul doesn't say we are to be thankful *for* every circumstance but *in* every circumstance.

We can be thankful in all things, recognizing that God is sovereign and unfailing in His faithfulness. In his book *Celebration of Discipline* Richard Foster says, "Scripture commands us to live in a spirit of thanksgiving in the midst of all situations; it does not command us to celebrate the presence of evil."

When I'm tempted to despair over any situation, I try to remember Paul's admonition to the Thessalonians (and to us) to give thanks. I pause to look around at God's beauty in the world, and to remind myself that

He is always offering beauty, hope, courage, and joy—good reasons for thanksgiving.

The Bible tells us, "Every good and perfect gift is from above, coming down from the Father of the heavenly lights, who does not change like shifting shadows" (James 1:17). God is pleased when we thank Him for His gifts. He delights in giving good gifts to His children. And he delights in our thanksgiving and praise to Him for all His goodness to us.

"Ancient Israel was commanded to gather three times a year to celebrate the goodness of God," says Richard Foster. "Those were festival holidays in the highest sense. They were the experiences that gave strength and cohesion to the people of Israel."

When we find ourselves lacking in desire to be thankful, we might meditate on the words of the song "Count Your Blessings," written by nineteenth-century Johnson Oatman, Jr.:

> When upon life's billows you are tempest-tossed,
> When you are discouraged, thinking all is lost,
> Count your many blessings, name them one by one,
> And it will surprise you what the Lord hath done.
> Count your blessings, name them one by one;
> Count your blessings, see what God hath done;
> Count your many blessings, name them one by one;
> Count your many blessings, see what God hath done.

45

The Therapy of Thanksgiving

*Give thanks to the LORD, call on his name; make known
among the nations what he has done. . . . Remember
the wonders he has done (Psalm 105:1,5).*

A schoolteacher took an underprivileged
little boy to a nature reserve. They
walked around for a while, saying little.
Finally his teacher asked, "What do you think?"

Without hesitation the boy replied, "We need to say
thank you for life."

We need to often say thank you to God not only for
life but for all of our blessings. If we read regularly from
the book of Psalms, we are reminded to give thanks.
Recently I was particularly impressed as I read Psalm
105 from the Amplified Bible. It begins, "O give thanks
unto the Lord, call upon His name, make known His
doings among the peoples! Sing to Him, sing praises to
Him; meditate and talk of all His marvelous deeds and
devoutly praise them."

What could I do but stop reading and meditate on
God's goodness and praise Him? Too often, instead of

remembering His marvelous deeds and thanking Him, I remember the things I'm displeased with, such as the disappointments that come.

It would be a good practice if we would remember in our conversations with friends to "talk of all of His marvelous deeds" rather than talking about all the bad that goes on in the world. We would be much happier and healthier. Maybe we need to work on training our minds to dwell on the goodness of God and the positive things our lives are filled with.

One minister suggested that we practice the therapy of thanksgiving. He says that if we list all our blessings, we will get a new understanding of the goodness of God.

Some families use the "gratitude bowl" as a reminder to be thankful. Everyone in the family writes down various things they're thankful for and drops the list into the bowl. During dinner the lists are taken from the bowl and read. Everyone is reminded of specific blessings to be thankful for.

Sometimes we get so "spiritual" that we forget to thank God for *material* things as well as for the spiritual ones. We could take a lesson from little children. If you're around young children, you know how they thank God for every little blessing, from the pajamas they wear to the beds they sleep in. Let's never become so sophisticated that we forget to heed Jesus' words to "become like little children."

The great American philosopher Henry David Thoreau said that every human being ought to thank God every day for being born. If we think it senseless to be thankful for being born into a world so full of troubles, we need to remember that God allows difficulties in our lives to strengthen us.

When I'm discouraged or feeling as if I'm getting nowhere toward accomplishing my goals, I usually turn to the Psalms and find a passage that speaks to me. Psalm 103:2 says, "Praise the Lord, O my soul, and forget not all his benefits." If I focus only on my feelings, I may not remember any of His benefits. But when I focus on the unchanging nature of God, I can readily thank Him.

Giving thanks to God in all circumstances motivates us to look for God's purposes in our lives and develops a stronger trust in God. Giving thanks is essential in order for us to rejoice. It focuses our attention upon God rather than our circumstances.

Some time ago in a magazine a man asked, "Why are we not more thankful?" Then he answered, "Thanksgiving is the product of careful cultivation. It is the fruit of a deliberate resolve to think about God, ourselves, and our privileges and responsibilities. . . . Material things do not dictate the horizons of our souls."

The Pilgrims knew well the truth of that last statement. More than 375 years ago they set an example of thanksgiving. They had few material blessings to be thankful for. The ship that brought them to America had no heat or plumbing. After more than two months of difficult sailing, they landed at Plymouth Rock in what is now Massachusetts. William Bradford wrote in his diary that they fell on their knees and thanked God for bringing them safely across the ocean.

In spite of hardships, they didn't complain or give

up. They trusted in God and found their fulfillment in Him. Their lives had purpose. They held on to their vision of making a new life for themselves and serving God in a new country.

The first winter in Massachusetts killed almost half of the colonists. But hope remained strong in the hearts of the survivors. The corn harvest brought special encouragement. In the winter of their second year, the colonists celebrated the first Thanksgiving Day. Governor Bradford decreed that a day be set aside for feasting and prayer, expressing thanks to God for His blessings.

I'm glad we still honor that custom. But let's make it more than just a once-a-year custom. Let's take time *today* to remember how blessed we are!

Words
of
Peace

46

Receiving God's Peace

Glory to God in the highest, and on earth peace to men on whom his favor rests (Luke 2:14).

The message proclaimed by the angels to the humble shepherds on the hillside is for you and me. Jesus came that we might have joy and peace regardless of our circumstances.

It was in the stillness of the night that the shepherds heard the angelic chorus. The Prince of Peace can give His peace to us only as we are open to receive it. Our busiest times are our most needful times to be quiet and receive the Lord's peace. The psalmist, inspired by the Holy Spirit, wrote, "Be still, and know that I am God." Often it is necessary for us to *discipline* our minds to be still.

Jeremiah wrote, "The LORD is good to those whose hope is in him, to the one who seeks him; it is good to wait quietly for the salvation of the LORD. . . . Let him sit alone in silence" (Lamentations 3:25,26,28). Jeremiah's point is that the goodness of the Lord can be best manifested to us when we seek Him in the stillness of our hearts.

It was in a "still small voice" that Elijah heard the voice of the Lord. It was when Samuel had lain down to quiet sleep that he heard the voice of the Lord calling him. When we quiet ourselves—spirit, soul, and body—the Lord is able to get through to us.

The pressures of work, or from simply living in a broken world, often make it difficult to be still. You may sit down to read your Bible and have a quiet time with the Lord, but thoughts whirl around in your head, and you find yourself struggling to be still.

The Savior knows all about that and He can help you. Because He lived on earth in human form, He understands our weaknesses and is able to supply our every need. He is always with us. *Emmanuel,* one of the names given to Jesus, means *God with us.* If we were more conscious of His being with us, we would find it easier to be still in His presence and receive the peace He came to give us.

A speaker said that for a long time he didn't understand peace. He kept waiting for it to fall on him like "a soft blanket of heavenly dew." But it never did. He eventually found that "peace doesn't just happen." He had to "make it happen" with God's help.

Peace doesn't offer us a world without storms; it provides security in the *midst* of life's storms. Peace, of course, begins at the cross, accepting Jesus as Savior and letting Him be our peace. Before Jesus left the earth He promised, "Peace I leave with you; my peace I give you. I do not give to you as the world gives. Do not let your hearts be troubled and do not be afraid" (John 14:27).

The peace proclaimed to the angels on the hillside that first Christmas night is for you and me. Let's receive it.

47

The Joy of Jesus

The angel said to them, "Do not be afraid. I bring
you good news of great joy that will be for all the
people. Today in the town of David a Savior has been
born to you; he is Christ the Lord" (Luke 2:10,11).

I can imagine how the teenage Mary must
have felt as she set out on a donkey with
her young husband, Joseph, on the 80-mile
journey to Bethlehem. She knew, of course, that the
time for delivery of her baby was near. No relative,
nurse, or midwife would be present with her.

The angel Gabriel had told Mary that her child
would be named *Jesus*, meaning *Savior*. Mary could have
thought, "This doesn't seem right. If my child is the
Son of God, I should have a better place to lay Him
than a straw-filled manger."

The circumstances of the first Christmas in
Bethlehem were not what you or I would have chosen
for the birth of the Savior. His mother, Mary, was as
human as you and I are. She must have felt lonely and
disappointed. But God chose it to be so. Now we look

back in wonder and awe as we celebrate the lowly birth of our Savior.

The world was unfeeling toward what was going on that night. Only some humble shepherds on a hillside knew that an extraordinary event had taken place, for God sent an angel to proclaim the good news. And the shepherds hurried off to Bethlehem to see the Christ Child.

Only a small percentage of the world's population knew or cared what happened on that memorable night. But you and I know it was the most significant event in human history, for Jesus came to bring us true joy. Let us enter into that joy!

48

The Calm in Our Hearts

*The light shines in the darkness, but the darkness has
not understood it (John 1:5).*

On the holy night when Christ was born, the
star shone brightly over the stable. With the
wonder of that scene etched in his mind,
Joseph Mohr wrote, "Silent night, holy night. All is
calm, all is bright. . . ."

No one would suggest that all is calm or bright in
our world today. But you and I can say, "All is calm, all
is bright in our hearts because the light of Christ shines
in our innermost beings." No one who lives in spiritual
darkness can understand that fact, but you and I can,
because we are indwelt by Christ.

I read a story about two men standing on a street
corner during the Christmas season, waiting for the
signal light to change. One of them impatiently grum-
bled about the holiday traffic. The other responded
happily, "I think it's fascinating to realize that a baby
born halfway around the world can create a traffic jam
in our city 2000 years later."

The Lord who triumphed over the forces of evil now lives in us to help us triumph over any negative or impatient attitudes or any forces that might be holding us in darkness. When Zechariah, the father of John the Baptist, prophesied concerning Jesus, he said, "Because of the tender mercy of our God, by which the rising sun will come to us from heaven to shine on those living in darkness and in the shadow of death, to guide our feet into the path of peace" (Luke 1:78,79).

Like a lamp turned on in a dark room is the presence of God's gift to us in the Person of Christ. He heals our hurts, calms our fears, turns despair into hope, and changes night to day. When our night is darkest, He shines the most brightly.

Paul tells us, "God, who said, 'Let light shine out of darkness,' made his light shine in our hearts to give us the light of the knowledge of the glory God" (2 Corinthians 4:6). Now that we have His light within us, it shines out through us to others.

We may not have chosen our current situation any more than Mary would have chosen a stable for the Savior's birthplace. But just as surely as God knew and cared about the events of that night, He knows and cares about us right now. His joy is for us today.

49

The Perfect Gift

*Mary treasured up all these things and pondered
them in her heart (Luke 2:19).*

The Christmas season is a special time of year. It's the time when most of us think about the gifts we want to give to those we love. We try to select gifts that have special meaning and express our appreciation for each individual. We wrap each gift with special care. We bring out the candles and other decorations, put up a tree, and do all the Christmasy things we've done over the years.

Of course, gifts and candles and trees and decorations don't make Christmas, but such things are pleasant tokens of the joyful season when we celebrate the birth of our Savior.

There's no evidence that gift-giving is a divinely appointed means of celebrating the Savior's birth. But since Christmas is the time we celebrate God's love gift to us, it seems appropriate that we express our love to those we love by giving to them.

We want to give good gifts. But however hard we try, we can never give a perfect gift. Only God could do that. When He gave us Jesus, He gave us the perfect gift for our past, for our present, and for all our tomorrows. He is the perfect gift for all our sins, all our problems, and all our hopes for the future.

I like to give presents of lasting value, but every material gift will depreciate in value as time passes. Not so with God's gift to us. The gift of His Son has ever-increasing value to us as we learn more about Him, and especially as we become better acquainted with Him. That is His desire for us—that we grow continually in a more intimate knowledge of Him. We do that as we read His Word daily and talk with Him continually. He rejoices when we, like children, celebrate His presence.

Once a year the Christian segment of the world celebrates in a special way Christ's presence and His coming. When God sent His Son, He foresaw the eventual worldwide celebration of the birth of His Son. Of course commercial celebrations miss the point of Christmas. But we need not let that keep us from honoring His birth or make of us another Scrooge. Let's never allow the prince of darkness to choke God's light within us.

Several years ago I received a letter from an acquaintance, urging me to give up celebrating Christmas, especially the use of a tree, "because the season began as a pagan feast." I answered her letter explaining our position as Christians and that a tree can remind us of the cross on which Jesus gave us the gift of eternal life. Joyful celebrations of the Savior's birth delight the heart of the Father.

It doesn't matter that no one knows the exact date of Jesus' birth or if pagans once corrupted the season. We can reclaim the season for what we know it is—a time to celebrate the holy birth of Jesus, our Savior, God's gift to all who will receive Him.

When we give gifts, we appreciate receiving thanks from the recipient. If our gift is one to be used over the years, it's nice to be thanked again in a few years. But too often I forget that God also likes to be thanked again and again for His gifts. It rejoices His heart when we praise and thank Him. The psalmist understood that well; David practiced giving thanks and praise to God as no one else ever has.

A fitting Christmas gift to our Lord might be to imitate David and resolve to thank Him every day for the gift of His Son and the many other signs of His love. His heart delights in our praise and our expressions of love. Praise can be the beginning of a more meaningful way to worship the Lord—our *gift* to Him.

You remember that as soon as the shepherds saw the star and heard the announcement of the angel that Christ was born, they immediately hurried off to Bethlehem. After seeing the Christ Child, the shepherds spread the word of what they had seen and heard. "But Mary treasured up all these things and pondered them in her heart."

It may be that the gift the Lord wants most from you and me is that we treasure up all these things and ponder in our hearts what we have been hearing and learning of Him all these years. As I read and meditate on God's Word, I realize more and more what a giver

God is. Whether we look within or without, we see that all we have, He has provided. What a reason to celebrate Christmas every day!

50

God's Joy in Our Lives

*The virgin will be with child and will give birth to a
son, and they will call him "Immanuel"—which means,
"God with us" (Matthew 1:23).*

It was Christmas morning, and our family
had gathered around the gleaming tree. All
eyes were focused on five-year-old Amy
while she tore the colorful wrapping from the box containing her special gift. Her blue eyes sparkled with joy
as she hugged her doll to herself. Our hearts sang with
hers when we saw how joyfully she received her gift.

The world's greatest gift—the One given in the
hope that the world would receive it with joy—was
announced 2000 years ago. Reflecting on that event
centuries later, Isaac Watts penned these words:

> Joy to the world! The Lord is come;
> Let earth receive her King;
> Let every heart prepare Him room,
> And heaven and nature sing.

The Savior came to enter our hearts, to bring us joy, to set us singing with the angels. Knowing He has given us His gift of salvation, how can our hearts do other than sing? The King born in Bethlehem has come to be born in us. He's more than a universal Being; He is our personal Savior—if we allow Him to be. His abiding presence enables us to rise to that level of joy with which the angels sang on that first Christmas day.

The Prince of Peace came that we might have peace *with* God—the peace that comes when we receive Him as personal Savior. But that's not all. He also wants us to have the peace of God—quietness and tranquillity in the midst *of* life's frustrations and pressures. That includes being at peace with ourselves, with others, and with our circumstances.

Jesus loves us so much that He left His heavenly throne to come and be born in human form. That same love prompts Him to dwell within us by His Spirit. Regardless of our circumstances, our relationship with Him can cause us to live in inner joy and peace at all times. Our awareness of His presence can play in our minds like quiet background music as we go about our daily activities.

The light that shone over Bethlehem's stable shines in our hearts to restore our joy and peace. Christmas is an ideal time for us to become childlike and renew our faith in the Lord and let Him be born anew in us.

Even as my family and I delighted over Amy's gleeful reception of her gift that Christmas morning, so our heavenly Father is delighted when we gratefully receive His gift of His Son. We cause His heart to sing with joy.

51

Star of Living Light

The shepherds returned, glorifying and praising God for
all the things they had heard and seen, which were just
as they had been told (Luke 2:20).

E very Christmas season we look with fresh
wonder at artistic scenes of the venerable
shepherds bowing in awe as the glory of the
Lord shone around them on that memorable night.
And we hear again with as much joy as when we first
read the angel's words: "Today in the town of David a
Savior has been born to you; he is Christ the Lord"
(Luke 2:11).

Then we read of how the shepherds left their flocks
and hurried off to Bethlehem and searched until they
found the newborn King. In that moment they knew
that nothing else was quite so important.

Another scene, old but always new, is that of the
wise men from the East following the star and asking,
"Where is He who has been born King of the Jews? For
we have seen His star in the East and have come to
worship Him. . . . And behold, the star which they had

seen in the East went before them, till it came and stood over where the young Child was. When they saw the star, they rejoiced with exceedingly great joy" (Matthew 2:2,9,10 NKJV).

It is significant that "when they saw the star they rejoiced." The wise men must have understood that the star symbolized the illumination which would come to the hearts of all who would accept Christ as Savior and Lord.

Quite likely they had read Micah's prophecy of the One who would be born in Bethlehem, and Isaiah's foretelling of the coming of the Prince of Peace. The star held such significance for the wise men that they never gave up following it. It seems likely that the journey took two years, since King Herod wanted to be sure he destroyed the Christ Child. He ordered that all the boys two years old and under be killed.

The wise men and the shepherds successfully arrived at the place where they found the Savior. But they didn't remain there. They returned home to spread the good news.

In our spiritual journey, there is no such thing as final arrival. We continue following the inner star, realizing that, like the word of prophecy of which Peter speaks, "it shines like a lamp amidst the darkness of the world, until the day dawns, and the morning star rises in your hearts" (2 Peter 1:19 PHILLIPS).

The wise men of the first Christmas followed a literal star. You and I have the Star, the Living Word, in our hearts to guide us. The wise men of old had each other's companionship on their journey. You and I have fellow members of the body of Christ to accompany us.

What we sometimes fail to realize is that all progress begins from within. In that sense, there are times when we travel alone. Those who realize this fact most fully are those who are being guided most clearly by the Star. Remember how Jesus denounced the Pharisees for their concern about externals while neglecting the inner life?

The One whose birth we celebrate came to set us free from the law of externals, to walk in the freedom of His love and life. We enter into that joyous freedom when we learn to look for fulfillment *within* instead of without. Jesus declared that the kingdom is within. Only in that inner kingdom is peace and joy.

Understanding deeply this truth of the kingdom was seventeenth-century Nicholas Herman, better known as Brother Lawrence. In one of his letters he counseled, "Let us enter into ourselves . . . because not to advance in the spiritual life is to go back. But those who have the gale of the Holy Spirit go forward even in sleep."

Being committed to the King of kings and Lord of lords, we learn not only to cultivate a sense of His presence during our waking hours, but also to fall asleep thanking Him for who He is and for His grace. In going to sleep with praise to Him, we "go forward even in sleep."

This is a good time to make a special effort to remember that the Lord is never far away. Having accomplished all that He did for us, He is with us and within us. Our salvation includes more than preparation for a future home in heaven. The Star shines in

our hearts to guide us, to protect us, to encourage us—
daily, nightly, hourly, moment by moment.

May the awareness of His presence be uppermost
in our thoughts. The Light of the world lives within us,
shining through us to illumine the path of others who
are not sure of the way to follow the star.

Many do not know that to follow the Star is to take
hold of life here and now. Perhaps our joy and tranquillity can be a light showing someone that life is
meant to be filled with the joy of the Lord.

52

God with Us

"They will call him Immanuel"—which means,
"God with us" (Matthew 1:23).

*I*mmanuel—God with us." Sometimes it takes a different kind of experience to bring us to an in-depth understanding of the truth that He really is with us. It happened to me one Christmas day several years ago.

A fresh gust of north wind hurled sleet and snow against my windowpane. I glanced out at trees draped with icicle daggers. Icy darkness would soon drive out the gray daylight, obliterating my view of the lawn upholstered in fluffy white.

The outdoor cold enhanced the cozy warmth inside. I had finished my Christmas shopping, decorating, and gift wrapping. An almost-thawed turkey waited in the refrigerator. The aroma of cookies and pumpkin pie wafted from my kitchen. Christmas carols floated through the air as I eagerly anticipated the arrival of my daughter, who was scheduled to fly to my home the next day.

For ten days an unsympathetic spell of subfreezing temperatures had gripped our area of Texas. Everyone hoped for a break in the weather. I turned on my television just in time to hear the newscaster announce that the ice storm had forced the airport to close. My hopes were dashed. There was no way my daughter could come home. I would spend Christmas alone.

It certainly won't seem like Christmas, I told myself. I had lived alone for nine years, but had never had to spend Christmas alone. I had always been with friends or family. *Could I handle it?*

I dropped onto the sofa and glanced out at the streets carpeted in white, as snow churned from the skies. I watched a small stray dog wade across my yard, chest deep in the fluffy snow, and my feelings of loneliness intensified.

My thoughts rambled. I remembered a recent letter from a friend, Ellen. She always looked forward to Christmas with the delight of a four-year-old. But not this year. With Christmas a little more than a week away, Ellen had not purchased a gift, put up a tree, or decorated a room.

"Christmas won't be the same this year," she wrote. "For almost a month I've done little but sit at the bedside of my hospitalized sister. But I'm realizing more clearly it's the spiritual meaning of Christmas that's most important. This experience is teaching me what I thought I already knew."

Could my experience teach me a needed lesson? Did I need a deeper grasp of the real meaning of Christmas? Was it possible that I had allowed my

Christmas to become little more than a time of decorating, baking, gift-exchanging, and family togetherness?

Traditions have helped make up my Christmas. There's nothing wrong with that, but perhaps it caused me to lose sight of the main focus. Was Christ still at the center?

A statement I had read said, "The shallow happiness of busy people often fills the place meant for the deep abiding joy of Emmanuel, God with us." I could only agree and ponder.

My daughter didn't come that Christmas. I spent Christmas alone—and yet not alone. I had a good day, one I'll never forget. Powdery whiteness continued to drift down. My water pipes froze. But a delightful warmth enveloped my heart. I had time to reconsider the real meaning of Christmas. I reread the Christmas story from Luke's Gospel and listened to Christmas carols. I felt the Lord's presence as I experienced Christmas, quietly celebrating the birth of Jesus in my heart.

Now I know that only one thing can keep Christmas from being Christmas for me—my failure to fully appreciate the purpose of the Savior's birth. The greatest joys of Christmas come not from giving and receiving, nor from being with my family, but from knowing more intimately the One whose birth we celebrate.